From Villain to National Hero

Chatoyer and the Early Struggle for the Independence of St. Vincent (Yurumein)

From Villain to National Hero:
Chatoyer and the Early Struggle
for the Independence of St. Vincent
(Yurumein)

©2019 Adrian Fraser

Published by **Hobo Jungle Press**
St. Vincent & the Grenadines, W.I.
Sharon, Connecticut, USA

First edition
August 2019

Printed in the United States of America

ISBN # 979-8-9922251-2-9

All rights reserved. No part of this publication may be reproduced, distributed, or transmitted in any form or by any means, including photocopying, recording, or other electronic or mechanical methods, without the prior written permission of the publisher, except in the case of brief quotations embodied in critical reviews and certain other noncommercial uses permitted by copyright law.

Cover Photograph: *Chatoyer (from the Obelisk at Dorsetshire Hill)*

From Villain to National Hero

Chatoyer and the Early Struggle for the Independence of St. Vincent (Yurumein)

Adrian Fraser

Dedicated to the 40th Anniversary of the Independence
of St. Vincent and the Grenadines

Contents

Glossary   ix

Acknowledgements   xi

Foreword   xiii

Preface   xvii

Chapter One: The Historical Literature   1

Chapter Two: Historical Context–The Kalinagos and the Early Resistance to European Efforts at Colonisation   13

Chapter Three: Chatoyer and the Continued Resistance to European Efforts at Control   25

Chapter Four: From Treaty to War   47

Chapter Five: The Final Showdown: The Death of Chatoyer and Exile of the Garínagu   61

Chapter Six: Epilogue: From Villain to National Hero   83

Final Note   99

Bibliography   101

List of Photographs

18th century map of St. Vincent   xvi

Restored Gun Powder Magazine at Owia   38

Northern Portion of St. Vincent
   Showing Carib Boundary Line   45

St. Vincent Actual Survey in 1733   60

Canon at Fort Charlotte   65

Tombstone in Anglican Church   82

The Right Excellent Paramount Chief, Chatoyer   95

Glossary

Indigenous Names	European Names	Current Names
	Berkshire Hill/Fort Charlotte	Fort Charlotte
	Calonery/Colonrie	Colonaire
	Canaan	Canouan
	Caribs/Charibbe/Charibbs/Caribbs/Charaib/Caribbees	Carib
	Chatoyer/Chatawae/Chatoyé	Chatoyer
Garifuna	Black Carib	Garifuna (Garinagu plural)
Kalinago	Yellow Carib	Kalinago
Massarica	South Union	South Union
Ouashegunny/Ouassigunny	Kingstown	Kingstown
Warrasaroo	Great Head/Arnos Vale	Arnos Vale
Washilabou	Cumberland	Cumberland
Yurumein	St. Vincent	St. Vincent and the Grenadines

Acknowledgements

The idea for this work emerged from a reflection on different questions that have been posed to me over the years about Chatoyer as national hero and about numerous discussions I have listened to, some not particularly well informed, about Chatoyer and the times in which he lived. It also represents an update of an extended essay I did at the time when Chatoyer was declared as our first national hero.

Any work of this nature can never be a singular effort and would have benefitted from the contribution of others.

The staff at the National Archives, especially Jeon Julien, was extremely helpful, even given the limitations of the Archives. The staff at the library of the University of the West Indies Open Campus allowed me easy access to books I needed.

I must express thanks to Dr Garrey Michael Dennie and Paul Lewis who read an early draft of this monograph and commented on it. Dr Joseph Palacio responded quickly to my request to him to do the foreword. He also made some useful suggestions.

As happens when one undertakes a project of this nature, family has to put up with periods of distraction, but it ultimately provides a sanctuary when one is occasionally forced to take periods of leave from the project and to re-energise oneself.

Presentations made to the annual conferences of the Garifuna Heritage Foundation also provided me with the opportunity to benefit from comments made and questions asked.

- Adrian Fraser

Foreword

In his monograph entitled "From Villain to National Hero: Chatoyer and the Early Struggle for the independence of St. Vincent" Adrian Fraser has contributed a timely review of the historical record around Joseph Chatoyer not only as a military strategist, but also as the persistent efforts of the people of St. Vincent to build the iconography of a national hero, thereby radically transforming the colonial perception of who can be elevated to the status of National Hero. Furthermore, Fraser postulates this unique promotion as setting the stage for the renewed independence of the nation of St. Vincent forty years after gaining its independence from Britain.

Fraser subdivides the historical component of his study into three phases: The first was the early Pre-Columbian era dominated by the Taino. The second was the painful series of endless wars among European colonial powers into which they inserted the indigenous peoples of St. Vincent and their neighbours. Finally, there was the war in St. Vincent in which Chatoyer took the leadership until his death in 1795. Shortly afterwards in 1797 the forced departure of over 2,000 Garifuna men, women and children to as far away as Roatan, Honduras, removed persons who had been eyewitnesses to the final atrocities they underwent as victims in their home country of St. Vincent before their exile.

More than 120 years after the war the process of transforming the cultural value system of St. Vincent to accept who had earlier been a villain and have him become a national hero is a major contribution of Fraser's monograph. The main problem becomes less the vestiges of colonial power than the challenges of building structures and systems embodying new sociocultural value systems consistent with a modern nation-state. Part of Fraser's contribution to this process has been to deliberately introduce terms and concepts in the monograph that resonate within the currency of modern-day indigeneity. For example, the people of St. Vincent are referred to as Garifuna or indigenous peoples and not Caribs. This is especially significant as earlier they had been referred to in such chromatic terms as "Yellow", "Red", or "Black" Caribs. My hope is that such relatively minor addition will be copied by other scholars in the Caribbean for vocabulary symbolism has its own contribution to cultural identity.

- Joe Palacio
Garifuna anthropologist (Belize)

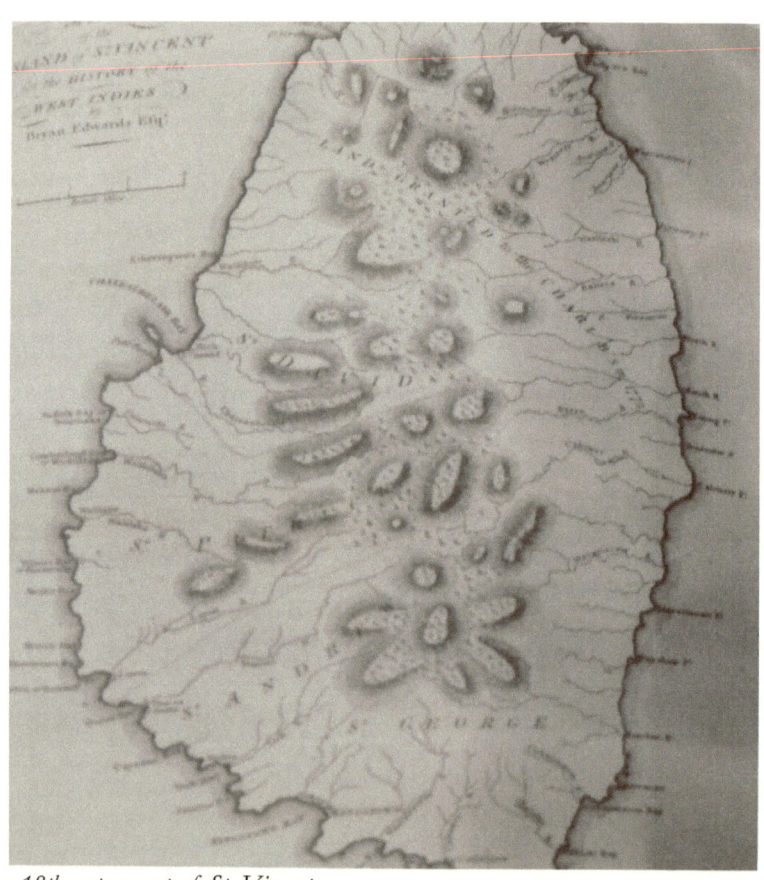

18th century map of St. Vincent

Preface

This year, 2019, St. Vincent and the Grenadines celebrates the 40th anniversary of its independence and the 17th year of the commemoration of Joseph Chatoyer as its first national hero. This publication is presenting the argument that October 27, 2019, is in fact the 40th anniversary of the recovery of the island's independence and Joseph Chatoyer was the leader of the early struggle for its recovery. St. Vincent first became a colony of Britain in 1763, although the British did not have full control of the fledgling colony. This came after a long period of struggle against the British, and French who had also sought the acquisition of the island. The early struggles against these efforts at control were led by the Kalinagos, labelled in the historical literature as 'Yellow Caribs'. By the first decade of the 18th century a new indigenous group, the Garifuna, which was the product of cohabitation between the Kalinagos and escaped African slaves, emerged.

The terms Kalinago and Garifuna are new to the literature. They are the names by which these people called themselves as opposed to those imposed on them by the Europeans and were widely used in the historical literature, where the Kalinagos were referred to as 'Yellow' or 'Red Caribs' and the Garifuna as 'Black Caribs'. When the Europeans arrived in this part of the world in 1492, they met two indigenous groups, the Taino in the northern Caribbean and the Kalinagos in St. Vincent and other countries of the 'Lesser Antilles'. It is believed by some archaeologists that Arawakan speaking peoples began colonising the 'Lesser Antilles' from about 400 BC. The Tainos of the Greater Antilles are believed to have originated from these Arawakan speaking peoples. From 400 AD the Igneri, another group of Arawakan speaking peoples dominated the 'Lesser Antilles'. These were commonly referred to as Arawaks. Between AD 1000 and 1400 the Kalinagos appeared in the Lesser Antilles, a short period of time before Columbus.

The Garifuna who are associated mainly with St. Vincent are believed, as stated earlier, to be the result of the intermixing of the Kalinagos and African slaves. The traditional story focused on the escape of African slaves who were shipwrecked off Bequia, an island of the Grenadines, in 1635 and who were assisted by the Kalinagos and taken by them to mainland St. Vincent. There is continuing debate about the date and the nationality of the slave ships originally believed to be Spanish. It is suggested that the ships were likely to have been Dutch rather than Spanish. The Slave trade started after 1517 following a plea by Las Casas to have African slaves replace Indian labour. The Kalinago people raided Spanish colonies in the north where they captured Indians and African slaves. A creole woman, Luis de Navarrete, who was captured in Puerto Rico and taken to Dominica described what she considered their frequent raids. She noted that "they have carried away a great quantity of negroes and left some in Dominica and distributed the rest among the Indians of these islands". She said that they boasted that "they had burnt and destroyed many farms...killed many people..." (p. 40 *Wild Majesty*). By 1700 Pere Labat, French missionary, who visited St. Vincent, drew attention to the number of Blacks living there, whom he described as escaped slaves from Barbados. The Garifuna joined the Kalinagos in the continuing struggle against British and French efforts to seize control of their country. By the mid-18th century they had become the numerically dominant group and then took control of the resistance to European efforts at domination. The Kalinagos continued the struggle but as a minor partner. The historical literature downplayed their role and pretended that they did not exist or if they existed were far removed from the struggle. This monograph seeks to inform readers of the important role played by the Kalinagos in those early struggles against European control.

It is the view here that Chatoyer as Paramount Chief, a title that seemed to be conferred in times of war, was leader of both the Garifuna and Kalinago peoples. In the discussion here about the 'Carib' wars reference is made mostly to the Garifuna because the two groups are treated as one people. This echoes a point made by Nancie Gonzalez; "My studies indicate that by the middle of the eighteenth century the 'Black Caribs' of St. Vincent were culturally and biologically indistinguishable from the so-called Yellow Caribs. Yet European observers, burdened by a racist imagination and ignorant of Mendelian genetics, insisted on distinguishing between darker, more combative Caribs and lighter more tractable ones – and in imposing policies that preserved the distinction" (p. 202-203, *The Garifuna of Central America*, Nancie L. Gonzalez).

St. Vincent only became a complete colony of Britain in 1797 when the majority of the indigenous population was sent into exile to Roatan, off Honduras, the majority being Garifuna. The period between 1763 and 1797 is therefore considered the period of the early struggle for the recovery of the country's independence despite the fact that the British did not control the total physical landscape.

This publication is grounded on the view that there is still a lot to be told and understood about the struggles of the Garifuna and Kalinagos, and particularly about the heroic ventures of Chatoyer and the people he led. This is particularly so since the citation read at the ceremony that proclaimed Chatoyer as national hero, referred to him as Kalinago and the people involved in the struggle as Kalinagos, ignoring the distinction that existed and the fact that he was of Garifuna extract. In 2007 a promise was made by Minister of Culture to have research done on the life of Chatoyer and to produce a documentary that she was going to try and have shown on the History and National Geographic channels (Address at March 14 ceremony, Sheron Garraway, *Searchlight*, March 16, 2007). This has so far not been realised, according to available information.

This publication is meant to update the knowledge we have of the struggles of Chatoyer and his people and to continue to question areas of the historical literature where the story told of the struggles was the story of the British, the victors, told from their point of view. Coming 17 years after Chatoyer's elevation to the status of National Hero it answers those who question Chatoyer's existence based on their view that the surname Chatoyer does not exist in St. Vincent. This is easy to answer since the overwhelming majority of the Garifuna people were sent into exile and at least one of his sons is recorded as having been part of those who were sent to Ruatan. Furthermore, anthropologist Joseph Palacio, in an interview with Mrs Felicita Francisco in Dangriga in Belize in 1997 was told that her grandmother reported to her what was told to her by her own grandmother, about one Gulisi "who claimed to have been born in St. Vincent to Chief Joseph Chatoyer and came to Honduras as one of the exiles" (p. 49, Palacio, *The Garifuna: A nation across borders*). Commentators at that time made mention of children of Chatoyer and a famous painting by Italian artist Agostino Bruinas, shows Chatoyer with five of his wives, one of them carrying a child, assumed to be Chatoyer's. There are also those who resent the idea of their national hero being dressed in loin cloth, failing to appreciate that he was an 18th century being, and that his people had their own culture, untainted in the beginning by European influence, and try to see him in the eyes of people of the 21st century.

This work has attempted to provide updated information and new perspectives on the struggles of our early peoples, but there are many unresolved questions given the fact that their story is still largely informed and influenced by the works of Charles Shephard and Sir William Young and by other British writers with their particular biases. Works of French missionaries and envoys are now more readily available. Despite their own biases we are able to produce different perspectives and create a better balance, remembering too, that their missionaries lived among the Kalinagos and the French had joined the Garifuna in their struggles against the British.

This is therefore a continuing story and part of the effort to recover our history and to see the Kalinagos and Garifuna, not merely as objects as depicted by colonial writers and commentators, but as subjects of their history, with a story that has not been fully told. The focus, as indicated earlier, is on Chatoyer as leader of the struggle of the people for recovering their independence. After the expulsion of the majority of Garifuna and Kalinago peoples, the British took full control of the colony and never gave it up until 1979. As we celebrate another anniversary, this monograph reminds us that the struggle started early. Chatoyer entered the historical literature in 1768, five years after the Treaty of Paris had sanctioned British control of the colony, and was at the forefront of the struggle until his death in 1795. His elevation to the status of first national hero is largely based on his role in the early struggle to recover the country's independence.

Although every effort was made to discard the name Carib, there are times when it has been used, often in emphasizing the joint role of the two groups, or for linguistic convenience. In the struggles after 1763, when the word Garifuna is used it accepts the view that the Kalinagos and Garifuna were one people and that the Kalinagos although few in numbers remained an essential part of the struggle.

Chapter 1
The Historical Literature

The traditional narrative and understanding of the struggles of Chatoyer and the Garifuna people against British efforts to take control of their lands and of the whole country was provided to us by advocates of the planting class and British colonial officials. They advocated for the rights of the British colonisers and portrayed the Garifuna as obstacles to British civilisation and in their view, by extension, progress. Two works have been very influential in shaping the thinking and generally the debate about the 18th century British–Garifuna conflict that led to two wars. The first written in 1795, entitled *An Account of the Black Charaibs in the island of St. Vincent's with the Charaib Treaty of 1773, and other Original Documents,* was by Sir William Young. The second, published in 1831 was Charles Shephard's, *An Historical Account of the Island of Saint Vincent.*

Who was Sir William Young? He was a member of parliament in Britain and had the same name as his father, William Young, who had been appointed to head the Land Commissioners following British entry into St. Vincent and their desire to sell the lands taken from the indigenous people. He served as governor of Dominica and had acquired some of the prized estates in St. Vincent. Sir William Young had served as one of the spokespersons for the West Indian planters in England and on the death of his father in 1788 had inherited his estates in St. Vincent. He edited his father's papers on the British 'Carib' conflict and published them in 1795 under the title listed above. That year 1795 was a time when the continuing conflict was heating up again with increased efforts by the Vincentian planters to have the "Caribs" removed from St. Vincent.

In examining Young's work we have to keep constantly in mind the fact that to some extent the actions of his father as Land Commissioner were responsible for the wars with the "Caribs". In 1793 in an article in the *Caribbean Quarterly* entitled "The Black Caribs – Native Resistance to British Penetration into the Windward Side of St. Vincent 1763-1773", Bernard Marshall stated that Young's work "which has completely distorted the picture has remained virtually unchallenged" (p. 5).

Its impact was recognised as early as 1807. In Bryan Edwards', *History of Civil and Commercial, of the British Colonies in the West Indies (vol. 2)*, he acknowledged having to correct views which he had expressed in an earlier edition about the attitude of the British Ministers to the indigenous people, after having been exposed to the views of Young. He stated; "The representation which I gave, had however the good effect of calling forth an historical account of those measures from my most respectable friend Sir William Young, Bart". He noted that Young's views were "founded on official papers and original documents in his possession and drawn up with all that candour and perspicuity which were to have been expected from its author's distinguished character and talent". He acknowledged that if the Crown's claim to St. Vincent and the lands of the people was 'just and valid' then he accepted that the measures they adopted to the native peoples were lenient and moderate. He admits, however, to being not fully convinced that the 'pretensions' of Great Britain were based on anything but political expediency. He was referring to Britain's claim against that of the Garifuna who had been in actual possession of the land. He quoted the Garifuna as having said that "they had originally been landed on the island by shipwreck and held it not only by right of conquest over the aborigines, but also by actual possession for near a century". He went on to explain that "Such was their title to St. Vincent's, and it would have been difficult, I think, for any nation in Europe to produce a better" (p. 422-425). Unlike some later British commentators on the issue Young had not entirely convinced Edwards in some areas. Edwards accepted, however, that future conduct of the Garinagu was to be tied to and determined by the treaty of 1773.

In 1956 in her historiography of the British West Indies, Elsa Goveia described Young's work as a "piece of settler history". She described it as being "full of the righteous indignation which inevitably prevailed at a time when the settlers found themselves threatened by the continued existence of a strong tribal enclave within the island" (p. 37). Written in 1795 when the conflict with the Garifuna people was coming to a climax, Young's purpose was to support the call for them to be removed from the island, citing "the constant 'perfidy' of the tribes, their strong attachment to the French, and their endemic hostility to the settler interest" (p. 37). In support of Goveia's view of Young's intent one can look at the last two pages of his book, where he states in an appeal to his home government, that without a strong hand by government, St. Vincent, which he regarded as " 'healthy, rich, and beautiful', might be lost to the Crown of Great Britain." He was supporting the island's council and assembly in the instructions they gave to their agent in London, "That the British planters, or the Black Charaibs, must be removed from off the island of St. Vincent's" (p. 124-125). She noted that the work was dedicated to Drewey Ottley who was the agent for the colony.

Marshall, in the article already cited, recognised Young's work as important despite what he considered its gross distortions, particularly because of the valuable source material, the original papers of his father. He argues, however, for a thorough examination of the "available data", and appeared to be pointing particularly to his view of the 'Black Caribs' as savages "whose sinister designs against the lives and properties of 'innocent' British subjects created a situation in which there was no alternative but to use force against them and remove them from the island at all costs" (p. 5). Marshall had indeed begun, if not continued, this process by looking critically at some of the views and conclusions of Young. The Peter Hulme and Neil Whitehead edited *Wild Majesty-Encounters with Caribs from Columbus to the Present Day*, emphasized too, that Young's work "clearly produced to serve the interests of the West Indian planters" in asking for the removal from the island of the "Caribs". Michael Craton described him as the least impartial of the planter historians, having 'mistold' the tale of the Vincentian Caribs (*Testing the Chains*, p. 146).

Charles Shephard's work was dedicated "to the Survivors of the Carib war, The Record of their Services, And of their Departed Companion in Arms..." He acknowledged that his work was undertaken at the request of the island's planting interest "who were anxious that the particular circumstances attendant on the Insurrection in 1795, should be preserved in a convenient form, and with more minuteness than has hitherto been done in the Historical Narratives of the West Indian Islands". They wanted their exertions, sacrifices and devotedness geared to their existence and that of their property to be recognised.

He made it known that his work was and "must necessarily" be a compilation and singled out the work of Bryan Edwards and

Thomas Coke's, *A History of the West Indies containing the Natural, Civil and Ecclesiastical History of Each Island* as the principal ones used. He claimed to have done so with considerable alterations since he had been able through the receipt of several manuscripts, diaries and other documentations of British survivors. He might have exaggerated the extent of alterations made, because especially in the case of the 2nd Carib War, he followed very closely, in many instances almost word for word, the narrative previously produced by Coke. A good example of this can be seen by looking at page 200 in Coke and 59 in Shephard. Coke states that a 'planter' from Marriaqua informed the Governor and Council that he had been warned by a 'neighbouring Charaibee' to leave the island because of an expected attack against the British. Shephard merely replaces 'planter' by 'merchant' and gives his name as William Greig. A large number of pages were copied directly from Coke, with only minor amendments.

Goveia describes Shephard's work as "an exercise in ex parte history", meaning of course that it was done in the interest of one side, as he admitted. While Young makes brief reference to the Second Carib War, Shephard covers it extensively.

Later commentators on the 'Carib Wars' have paid little attention to the work of Bryan Edwards and Thomas Coke. Coke stated his obligations to the works of earlier historians, "In a work like the present it must naturally be expected, that the writer will avail himself of every authority already extant. He should indeed deem himself highly culpable in omitting this; and, in fact, he will find it difficult, on many occasions, to avoid expressing himself, on the same common topics, in nearly the same language as his predecessors" (Vol. 2, p. 13). Among the historians mentioned was Bryan Edwards, "to whom the palm of superiority may be justly assigned".

Edwards in his view had one major omission, that is, of not paying enough attention to the religious missions being set up in the islands. He would have been referring to the Methodist mission. He saw his writings as filling that gap in Edwards' work. What Coke says about Edwards could equally apply to Shephard as his work relates to Coke's, that is, finding it difficult "to avoid expressing himself, on the same common topics, in nearly the same language as his predecessors".

One major development in a re-examination of the work of Shephard is the greater availability of French accounts of the 1795 war. In *The Garifuna — A Nation Across Borders* that was edited by Joseph Palacio, he referred to the charting of new grounds in Garifuna history. He alluded to Peter Hulme's translation of French documents, "originally dating back to the latter years of the 18th century", the time of the Carib wars. Palacio also, through the medium of oral history, "narrates part of a folklore that had remained for over 200 years within a family in Dangriga, Belize, about a woman who came across from Honduras to Dangriga with her sons. Palacio's informant was the granddaughter of the granddaughter of the protagonist, who was reportedly the daughter of Chatoyer. Her name from St. Vincent was Gulisi. She shared bits of information about her life in St. Vincent as well as in Honduras before coming to Belize" (p. 12).

Hulme in his article in the publication, "French accounts of the Vincentian Caribs" (translated and introduced by Peter Hulme), comments on the fact that with the removal of the "Caribs" from St. Vincent, "the only voices who wanted to tell the story, their story of suffering and eventual triumph, were the British planters and their allies." Perhaps it might be more accurate to say that they were the only persons in a position to do so. Hulme echoes a point made by Marshall, although his was pointed at William Young, that "the planters' version of the ethnography of the Vincentian Caribs entered the historical record, where it has never been seriously challenged", and "have become historical truth" (p. 21- 22).

Hulme expressed the importance of the works he was introducing, "two previously ignored French voices into the debate about the nature and constitution of Carib society and culture in the Windward Islands and particularly on St. Vincent during the eighteenth century". The works were Marquis de Lambertye, *History of the Caribs: A Savage Nation Living on the Windward Islands of America and Part of the Mainland* and Moreau de Jonnès, *Adventures in Wars of the Republic and Consulate.*

For the purpose of heightening our understanding of the 2nd Carib War, Hulme noted, "Moreau's friendship with the Caribs during a time of war undoubtedly led to greater intimacy and arguably, therefore, to greater knowledge. During those months at the end of 1795, Moreau certainly lived in much closer daily contact with the Vincentian Caribs than any other outsider at this time, possibly during the whole course of the eighteenth century" (p. 25).

He admits to possible bias from the French source just as is recognised with the British sources. What is important to this publication is the involvement of the Kalinago people in the 2nd Carib war, a point emphasized by Moreau. British sources had downplayed this since it was important to their story to see the war as primarily one fought by the Garifuna whom they claimed, had seized the lands of the Kalinagos. One of the issues raised by William Young was that of what he termed the superiority of the British claim, something to which, as was seen earlier, Bryan Edwards had responded.

Other works in more recent times have taken issue with some aspects of the accounts of the two English authors, particularly their conclusions about the end of the First Carib War and about who provoked the conflict that led to the wars and matters relating to the death of Chatoyer. Some of these works include *The Rise and Fall of the Black Caribs*, written in 1972 by I E Kirby and C I Martin. They tried to retell the narrative from the point of view of Vincentian nationalists but were limited by the data available to them. Kirby, as an archaeologist, was able to put more precision to the narrative. They accepted Young's version of the death of Chatoyer, but Kirby later backed away from that and questioned the version given by Young.

One contemporary account of the two 'Carib' wars that appeared to have been written about 1800 should be mentioned. Alexander Anderson's *Geography and History of St. Vincent, West Indies*, had been unpublished and left in the library of the Linnean Society of London until it was edited and transcribed by Richard A and Elizabeth S Howard in 1982. Anderson, unlike Shepherd and Young, had not written to defend the planting interest. He was in support of British colonialism but was at times critical of the attitude of the British. He saw flaws in the 1773 Treaty and decried the approach of the colonists following the treaty, blaming them to some extent, for the outbreak of war in 1795. He was, however, no friend of the "Caribs".

As he stated, "I mean not to exculpate the Caribs of their rebellion and unheard of cruelties... They were not an ignorant people — from their long communication with Europeans they were far more intelligent than any other race of savages but unfortunately, the information they thus acquired — rendered them more dangerous, as all they have been taught were the cunning and deceit of Europeans with many of their vices" (p 61-62).

Anderson lived in St. Vincent during the 1795 war, having taken up the position of second director of the botanical garden in 1785. He knew the country very well as he went about collecting plants and even dialoguing with the "Caribs" about medicinal plants. He was the first person known to have climbed the Soufriere volcano. Since his work was published only thirty-seven years ago it would not have had any impact on the earlier debate on the British- Garifuna conflict and struggles.

Among the other works providing different perspectives on the Carib–British situation was Robin Fabel's *Colonial Challenges- Britons, Native Americans, and Caribs 1759-1775*. He compared British treatment of the "Caribs" with that of the Cherokees of the Mississippi delta. He described his work as a study of non-white residents of British colonies "who had, or acquired, grievances against the Crown". The work, he stated, was "about the peoples of the Cherokee homelands, the delta of the Mississippi, the island of St. Vincent, and about the way the British conducted relations with them" (p. 1). The section on St. Vincent is taken up largely with the First Carib War and ends soon after the war.

He seemed to have made exhaustive use of records in the British Library, Public Records Office, the Colonial Office, and Library of Congress, thus answering Marshall's call for an examination of the available data. He looked at the British political environment to show the impact it had on what was happening among some of the native peoples in the colonies, including the Black Caribs. His discussion of the origin of the Carib–English conflict is quite informative and differs in a number of ways from the accounts given by Young.

In Michael Craton's *Testing the Chains–Resistance to Slavery in the British West Indies*, 1982, he incorporates the 2nd Carib War in St. Vincent in what he referred to as "Slave Resistance in the Age of Revolution". The chapter "The Storm Breaks: Grenada and St. Vincent, 1795" links the Fedon rebellion, which involved the free coloureds and slaves with the Carib struggles. It should be pointed out too, that slaves were used by the British in St. Vincent against the Garifuna, while escaped slaves, and free coloureds and slaves from the French islands joined the struggle in St. Vincent against the British. The start of the Fedon rebellion in Grenada sparked the war in St. Vincent, something that was not coincidental but had to do with French involvement in both struggles.

Hilary Beckles' "Kalinago (Carib) Resistance to European Colonisation of the Caribbean" in *Caribbean Quarterly*, December 2008, *Crossroads of the Empire–The European–Caribbean Connection* 1492-1992, guest edited by Sir Roy Augier, sought to give a fresh look to the Kalinago resistance. While we have been concentrating a lot on Chatoyer and the Garifuna struggles against the British, it must not be forgotten that the struggle against European encroachment in the area started with the Kalinagos. The Garifuna were able to build on this, but they took control as the numerically dominant group at the time when the British began their colonisation of St. Vincent.

The most recent publication, 2012, was Christopher Taylor's *The Black Carib Wars–Freedom, Survival, and the Making of the Garifuna*. Taylor used the archives in the United Kingdom, France, St. Vincent and the Grenadines, and the British Library. He seemed to have done extensive work utilising Colonial Office documents, War Office files and existing secondary data. It is indeed a very informative study of the 'Black Carib Wars.'

My 2002 monograph *Chatoyer (Chatawae) National Hero of St. Vincent and the Grenadines* was, as indicated then, an extended essay done in preparation for the celebration of the First National Heroes Day and meant to provide information to the public that knew little about Chatoyer despite the long period of advocacy calling for his elevation to the status of National Hero. I raised some issues then, particularly questions about the account of Chatoyer's death, and introduced the earlier recognition of Chatoyer in New York in 1823 with the play the "Drama of King Shotaway." We have been seriously handicapped by the non-existence of copies of the play and have only been provided with the Playbill that informed us about the play.

The reconstruction and retelling of the struggles of the Kalinagos, Garifuna and of Chatoyer, Paramount Chief, is a continuing one since we are still faced with the fact that the early works of Young and Shephard had for a very long time shaped our thinking on the history of our early peoples and their struggles with the Europeans. More exhaustive work perhaps still needs to be done, with a look at more documentation from the French and Spanish archives.

Chapter 2
Historical Context: The Kalinagos and Early Resistance to Europe Efforts at Colonisation

When Columbus and the Spaniards arrived in the region in 1492 the Kalinagos resided in and were in control of St. Vincent. It is not known if the Spaniards ever visited the country during that early period. The name 'Point Espagnol' in the north eastern part of the country suggests a Spanish connection but the Spaniards who accompanied Columbus were known to name countries just by sighting them. At one time the country celebrated January 22 as a holiday said to be named as the day in 1498, on his fourth voyage, when Columbus 'discovered' the country. It is now known that on January 22 of that year Columbus was still in Europe, not having left as yet on his 4th voyage. That holiday is no longer in existence, but the decision to discontinue it generated political turmoil.

The Kalinagos were the last group of migrants to have settled St. Vincent and the Lesser Antilles before the arrival of the Europeans. They are believed to have arrived here about 1,000 AD and to have been preceded by the Taino who had by then moved to the northern Caribbean. Arawakan speaking peoples began colonising the Lesser Antilles from about 400 BC. The Taino peoples are said to have been related to these Arawakan speaking peoples. From AD 400, the Igneri, another group of Arawakan--speaking peoples dominated the Lesser Antilles. These were commonly referred to as Arawaks in the historical literature. Between AD 1000 and 1400 the Kallinagos appeared, a short period before Columbus.

The absence of gold and the fierce resistance of the Kalinagos, who were able to master the use of the jagged landscape of Dominica and St. Vincent, kept the Spanish away. One historian stated that, "From the first landing to the end of his days gold obsessed Columbus, directed his explorations and dominated his conduct" (Sauer, p. 23). Some historians have also pointed to their 'nomadic nature' and existence of small communities as an inhibiting factor (Beckles, 1992, p. 4). Columbus drew a distinction between the peaceful Taino and the ferocious Caribs (Kalinagos) whom he considered cannibals. The Taino communities in the northern islands that endured most of the Spanish attacks were occasionally assisted by Kalinagos from the southern colonies. They raided plantations and Spanish ships, taking away African slaves and Tainos. Fabel drew attention to this: "The Caribs in the seventeenth century were strong, assertive, and bellicose. From Dominica or St. Vincent, Caribs would assemble for ambitious expeditions against common enemies. Their seagoing canoes could range as far as 300 miles from St. Vincent. Such exploits infuriated British colonial authorities, not merely because of the Caribs' prowess in warfare, which was considerable, but also because their activities worked to the benefit of the French."

With a decline in the Indian labour supply in the northern colonies, the Spanish turned their attention to the southern islands in search of labour. In 1503 the Queen had authorised that the Kalinagos could be taken as slaves. A Royal decree of July 3, 1512, designated "Caribs" as subject to capture because of their resistance to Christians. St. Vincent was identified as one of those islands. In fact, islands from Dominica to Tobago were singled out (Sauer, 193). The African slave trade had officially started from 1517 after Las Casas's plea to have Indian labour replaced by that of Africans. Resistance in the northern colonies by the Taino and Kalinago peoples had been virtually crushed by the end of the 16th century. The Leeward islands and Barbados had become victims of Spanish attacks with the result that St. Vincent and Dominica emerged as the base for Kalinago resistance.

French missionary Père Labat who visited Dominica and St. Vincent in 1700 wrote about the fighting skills of the Caribs, complementing what was quoted earlier from Fabel. The Carib children, he noted, learnt to shoot with bows and arrows at an early age. "They appeared to take no aim but very seldom missed…though they fire very quickly…(and) can loose ten or a dozen arrows in the time it takes to load a gun" (p. 111-112). Their skills continued when they were exposed to guns. Accounts exist of Kalinago attacks on Spanish colonies in the north. As indicated earlier, a creole woman, Luisa de Navarrete, captured in Puerto Rico in 1576 and taken to Dominica, reported on raids where Africans were taken away and distributed among the southern islands. Raids were also made on Spanish ships. With Spanish concentration on the northern islands and their perceived success, the smaller islands attracted the attention particularly of the Dutch, English and French and led, at first, to privateering activity in the 16th century. Illicit trading also developed, particularly by the Dutch, who by the early 17th century presented the most formidable challenge through their trading activity, to what was then a Spanish monopoly. Early attempts at settlement were made on the Guiana coast of South America. The fearsome and well- known resistance of the Kalinagos and their alleged cannibalism that had been falsely spread by the Spaniards seemed to have inhibited attempts to enter St. Vincent.

Lawrence Keymis, an English seaman on a voyage to Guiana in 1596, encountered Kalinagos from St. Vincent. The seamen were promised stores but were very suspicious of that offer and felt that they were delaying them with the intention of finding an opportunity "to betray, take and eate us, as lately they had devoured the whole company of French shippe...". The ship, Olive Branch, in 1606 reported on its arrival near to the shore of St. Vincent, "which puts us all in great feare, for if God had not sent us a gale from the shoare, we had runne a ground, and we had had all our throats cut by the Indians of that island" (*Wild Majesty*, pgs. 57-58, 64).

The early attempts at settlement on the Guiana coast proved unsuccessful and led to efforts in the smaller Caribbean islands where it was hoped that tobacco could be provided for a growing market in Europe. The earliest recorded attempt of Europeans being in St. Vincent came from a Dutch source and occurred in 1634. The report quoted by Van Der Plas from W R Menckman-De Nederlanders in het Caraibische Zeegebied, 1942, p. 43, stated that a Dutch ship on a voyage to Curacao, got to St. Vincent to 'refresh their ships' "but as they found ample time to build a few smaller landing craft necessary for the occasion they stayed in Cumberland Bay, then called Washilabeu..." Unfortunately, Van Der Plas provides us with no further information especially about the people they might have met. Apart from this 1634 visit the other Europeans who came early to St. Vincent were French missionaries, with the arrival of Fr. André Dejan in 1652, followed by the first resident missionary Fr. Guillaume Aubergeon in 1653.

Between 1624 and 1632 the British took control of St. Kitts, Barbados, Nevis, Antigua and Montserrat. The early English settlers in St. Kitts in 1624 made accommodation the next year with French settlers in face of possible Carib attacks. The French next settled in Martinique, Guadeloupe, Grenada, and St. Lucia in 1650.

The introduction of sugar cultivation into Barbados and the Leewards demonstrated the enormous potential of the British Islands and the benefits of trade. The French also got into the cultivation of sugar in Martinique, Guadeloupe, and St. Domingue. St. Vincent and Dominica resisted European settlement until the latter part of the 18th century. Kalinago attacks on English settlements as seen with Antigua in 1640 increased the resentment of the British and French against them and led to efforts to have them evicted and, if possible, exterminated. Additionally, with the enormous profits made from cultivating sugar, land in St. Vincent and Dominica became a strong temptation for planters who wanted to expand their cultivation of sugar and others who urgently sought to get into it.

Efforts at English and French settlement in St. Vincent presented the greatest challenge to the Kalinagos as it did to those in the other Windward Islands and the remainder of the Lesser Antilles. By the middle of the 16th century the number of African escaped slaves in St. Vincent continued to grow although they were still outnumbered by the Kalinagos. Their combined military expeditions against the French and English reinforced the determination of the English and French who were desperate for virgin lands held by the Kalinagos. They resented, too, the attacks on their settlements in the Leeward Islands. Van der Plas described St. Vincent as the headquarters of Carib activities and stated that when any of the neighbouring islands was in trouble they appealed to the Vincentian

Caribs for assistance. The Vincentian Caribs he claimed, "had some huge pirogues, ready to transport hundreds of warriors to any island, from Tobago to Antigua" (p. 6).

The period of the 1630s and 1640s was particularly bad for French–Kalinago relations. Following defeats suffered in attacks on Guadeloupe in 1634 and Martinique in 1635, the Kalinagos were prepared to hit back and to attack their existing settlements. This affected even the efforts of the French missionaries that were beginning in some parts of the region, particularly Martinique. The capture of "Caribs" by a French ship off Dominica for possible sale as slaves inflamed the Kalinagos. Two "Caribs" were captured by a French man and sold as slaves in Tortuga. General de Poincy, governor general of the French Caribbean, who was cautious about possible Kalinago attacks, ordered that the Caribs be returned. Very grateful for this the Caribs were sent to St. Kitts to thank the general, who had an interest in having them converted to Christianity. There they met the French missionary Pere Aubergeon, who was quite familiar with the Kalinago language. He must have impressed them and was invited to come to St. Vincent. He arrived in 1653, following a brief visit to Martinique and was joined not long after by Pere Gueimu. The heated feelings against the French by the Kalinagos persisted. The efforts at settlement by the French continued to enrage them. Van der Plas noted the call for war against the French that began in 1654. This was stimulated by the report of a young "Carib" who was badly treated by a French captain, who suspected him of killing one of their crew off St. Vincent. He escaped to St. Vincent. The number of incidents had reached a boiling point and there was a call for war against the French that affected even the missionaries who had lived among them. The big explosion came in St. Vincent when the "Priest House", believed to have been established in Barrouallie — but could well have been Buccament — was invaded and the two missionaries and two French men sharing in their work had been killed. This seriously set back French missionary activity for a while, and even when it resumed the attention shifted from purely Carib to incorporate the African slaves who had been increasing in numbers. The story of this incident is recorded in Van der Plas' *The History of the Massacre of Two Jesuit Missionaries in the Island of St. Vincent,* 24 January 1654, 1954. Van der Plas described this period as "one of the bloodiest revolts ever staged by the Caribs".

Even without being established on the island, the British and French were laying claims to the island. In 1627 Charles I's bold and brazen grant of the islands to the Earl of Carlisle included St. Vincent. Following his death, the grant went to Lord Willoughby in 1672. These grants were resisted by the Kalinagos. Their resistance to French claim to occupy some land based on a piece of paper that they said gave them rights to the land, was also noted by Abbe Raynalds (*Histoire Naturelle et Morale des Isles*, quoted by Van der Plas, p. 5). " I know not what that piece of paper says but read what is written on my arrow! My arrow does not lie, go away or I will burn your house tonight".

There were often disagreements among the colonial officials as to the approach which should be taken. Some favoured punitive attacks on the Kalinagos while others, especially those in the Leeward colonies who were often the victims of Kalinago retaliation, preferred dialogue. In 1667, March 23, a delegation from Willoughby in Barbados negotiated an agreement with the Kalinagos of St. Vincent, Dominica and St. Lucia. This did not work as they had hoped, for the arrival of colonists from Barbados to St. Vincent met with strong resistance and they were forced to escape from the island.

In 1686, Col. Edwin Stede, Lt. Governor of Barbados sanctioned a visit by Captain Temple to prevent French efforts to draw wood and water from the Island. This was despite a 1660 act of neutrality by the French and British that acknowledged the Kalinago rights over the land. The French, however, were allowed to settle on parts of the Leeward coast by the Caribs. It was clear they had some understanding of the geopolitics of that time and of the French–English rivalry. They considered the British as the greater threat because of their focus on the acquisition of land. The French who began to settle were engaged in small scale farming of tobacco and other minor crops that did not demand huge plantations and hence large land space. It is believed by some that apparent Kalinago–Garifuna/African conflict facilitated the entry of the French who were called on to assist the Kalinagos against the Garifuna who were growing in numbers. It is not clear at what point the Garifuna became numerically superior but Labat said in 1700 "the numbers of the negroes have increased to such an extent that they are more numerous than the Caribs and have compelled the latter to give them the windward side of the island" (p. 137).

In 1722 the grant of George I to the Duke of Montagu led to an expedition to St. Lucia and St. Vincent under Captain Uring. Captains Brathwaite and Orme were sent to St. Vincent after the failure of the expedition to St. Lucia. Fabel's account of that visit in his *Colonial Challenges–Britons, Native Americans, and Caribs 1759-1775*, using Calendar of State Papers, described the venture as an "expensive fiasco".

"At St. Vincent they received his representative, Captain Henry Orme, coldly. Armed only with bows, arrows, and clubs, they denied him water unless he paid for it and contemptuously rejected proffered gifts. They gave Orme no chance to discuss the bargain he was authorised to make: the rights of free-born British subjects in exchange for submission to the duke's government" (Fabel 147-148).

Captain Brathwaite's report on the proceedings as told to Captain Uring was given in more detail by Bryan Edwards. They were at first tricked into entertaining whom they were led to believe was the Indian General. They were subsequently taken to meet the real Indian General. He was told they were informed that they were embarked on establishing a settlement and were refused wood or water. On his return to the shore he met a number of negroes. (They always confused the Africans and Garifuna.) He later sent them presents of rum, beef, bread, and cutlasses. In return, two Indians were sent to thank them and assured them of having access to wood and water. They were encouraged to come ashore, and the two Indians were to be left as hostages. With Captain Watson, Brathwaite went ashore and found there one whom he described as the brother of the chief of the Negroes who had arrived with five hundred negroes. Brathwaite once again invited them on board his ship and left Captain Watson as a hostage, under their guard.

They were entertained with drinks of wine after which Brathwaite seized the opportunity to inform them of the reason for their visit. He reported their response: "They told me it was well I had not mentioned it ashore, for their power could not have protected me; that it was impossible; the Dutch had before attempted it but were glad to retire. They likewise told me, two French sloops had, the day before we came, been amongst 'em, gave 'em arms and ammunition, and assured them of the whole force of Martinico for their protection against us; …but declared they would trust no Europeans; that they owned themselves under the protection of the

French, but would as soon oppose to their settling amongst 'em or any act of force from 'em as us; as they had lately given an example, by killing several.... They advised me to think what they said was an act of friendship." Once Captain Watson had returned, they decided to take their leave (Edwards, p. 414-420).

No other serious effort at settlement seemed to have been made after 1723. But at the Treaty of Paris in 1763 the British were given control of St. Vincent, with the Kalinagos and Garifuna being, of course, not part of that decision.

Hilary Beckles reminds us of the Kalinago's "principal contribution to the Caribbean's anti-colonial and anti-slavery tradition" (1992, p. 13). They strongly protected their liberty and "national status" even at pains of death. Most formidable in this regard were those of St. Vincent and Dominica. Van der Plas argued that "The occasional show of friendship or alliance with the French, English or Dutch was merely a matter of expediency" (p. 8-9).

It is not clear when the Garifuna became the numerically dominant group and began to spearhead the protection of their land and the defence of St. Vincent. By 1723 with the visit of Brathwaite, Watson and Orme the Garifuna had clearly expanded their presence but had been collaborating with the Kalinagos, the leaders of both groups having been invited on board their ship and agreeing on a collective response to the British presence. They had, particularly in the latter part of the 17th century ,participated jointly in defending the country against European attempts at control. When the British took control of St. Vincent in 1763, it was reported there had been about 3,000 Garifuna, 4,000 French, including their slaves, and about 100 Kalinagos (William Young, p. 18). The Kalinago numbers had declined significantly through diseases, defending themselves against the Europeans and perhaps through conflicts with the Garifuna. Christopher Taylor did not consider conflict with the Garifuna of major significance, arguing that "there is little evidence of the sort of wholesale slaughter that would have been necessary to bring about such a dramatic demographic collapse of the former (Kalinagos) in relation to the latter" (p. 21).

It was the Garifuna who took charge of the struggle against the Europeans in the 18th century. By the second half of that century, circumstances and the nature of the struggle and strategies had changed. After 1763 it was no longer geared to preventing European settlement. The presence of the British from 1763 was a reality and they had to deal with that. This is the period when Chatoyer emerged and led the struggle.

We now turn our focus on Chatoyer and the Garifuna and the struggle which led to his death at the beginning of their final battle against the British in 1795.

Chapter 3
Chatoyer, the Garifuna and the Continued Resistance to European Efforts at Control

I have shown that the struggle against European attempts at colonisation began with the Kalinago people who were later assisted by the Garifuna, then numerically in a minority. So, what was new? It is not clear when the Garifuna became the dominant group numerically, although it is suggested that this manifested itself in 1723 when the two groups acted in unison to thwart efforts at colonisation by Captain Braithwaite. This was based on Brathwaite's report published in 1726 by Nathaniel Uring, on his failed expedition to establish a physical presence in St. Vincent on behalf of the Duke of Montagu. He claimed to have been met by the Kalinago leader and one hundred men while the "Negro" leader was accompanied by four hundred of his men. Even if this does not fully establish their dominance, based on figures supplied by the British when they took control of St. Vincent in 1763, there were 3,000 'Black Caribs' or Free Negroes, 4,000 French with their negro slaves and 100 "Red Caribs" (Young 18). It is the relative numbers that are significant for it indicates a significantly reduced Kallinago presence even considering that the British and French were often not precise about the distinction between Kalinago and Garifuna and Garifuna and free negroes. By then the Garifuna were the ones in charge even though the relationship between Garifuna and Kallinago still needs to be re-examined.

Of significance to the continued struggle against the Europeans, particularly the British, was the fact that the geopolitical situation had changed. The British were no longer an outside force attempting to establish control by professed claims given by British monarchs as patronage to favourites, especially those who had performed valuable services in their many wars in the 17th and 18th centuries. When those efforts failed, as we have seen before, they resorted to attacks on the indigenous forces.

The islands that constituted the Eastern Caribbean that had been populated either by the Kalinagos or the Tainos were considered by the Europeans to be part of the Spanish monopoly granted in 1494 when the Treaty of Tordesillas ratified the Papal Bull of Alexander VI. This had divided the colonies recently stumbled on by the Europeans, between the Spanish and Portuguese. By the 17th century the Dutch, English and French had begun to challenge the Spanish monopoly and had started settling on some of the islands from 1623. By the end of 1762 the only islands that had not come under English or French control were St. Vincent and Tobago, although there were French settlers in St. Vincent who realised, however, that they were there through the courtesy of the Kalinagos who had allowed them to settle on a portion of the western or leeward coast of St. Vincent and in designated areas. The earliest challenge was from the Dutch through their illicit trading and by English and French privateers. The settlements from 1623 were mainly by privateering interests and chartered companies. When the British and French began settlement of the colonies hoping to export, at first, tobacco and other tropical products and later sugar, they had to contend with the Dutch's hold on trade. Three Dutch wars eventually led to the dismantling of their control and to increased rivalry and war between the French and English with the Dutch often but not always siding with the British. What followed were wars that were described as wars of trade and empire (Augier). Most of these wars started over European conflicts on issues related to the balance of power in Europe, but often involved matters of trade and empire that took hold of Caribbean interests.

The wars that impacted on St. Vincent were the War of Austrian Succession, 1740-1748; the Seven Years War, 1756-1763; the War of American Independence, 1776-1783; and the French Revolutionary and Napoleonic War, 1793-1815. The Treaty of Aix-La-Chapelle that ended the War of Austrian Succession accepted that St. Vincent, Dominica, St. Lucia, and Tobago belonged neither to the English nor French, but recognised the reality that Dominica and St. Vincent were under the control of the Kalinagos. In fact, the act of neutrality was agreed on as early as 1660 (Shephard, p. 21). The Treaty of Paris at the end of the Seven Years War gave control of St. Vincent to the English. During the War of American Independence St. Vincent was occupied by the French in 1779 but returned to the English at the Peace of Versailles in 1783. The French Revolutionary and Napoleonic Wars created conditions in the Caribbean that prompted the Haitian Revolution and spurred revolts in Grenada and St. Vincent.

The year 1763 thus ushered in a new phase in the lives of the Garifuna and Kalinago peoples. St. Vincent was now fighting its own battles on its own turf. The role of the French after this has to be looked at. When the British took control some French people left, while others opted to remain. The challenge for the Garifuna was to defend territory that now had an English population occupying part of its country. Of course, the decision to hand control of St. Vincent to the English was done without acquiescence by the indigenous people. It was part of European arrogance that was central to their colonisation efforts and actions based on their claims to a superior civilisation and authority that supposedly gave them rights of control over native populations.

One senses that before 1763 the Garifuna, like the Kalinagos before, had some understanding of the geopolitics of that time. But after 1763 understanding the relationship between the English and French was critical to the strategies they adopted. They drew a distinction between the French who were small farmers in St. Vincent and the English who were motivated by the riches to be made from sugar, especially on virgin lands as those under their control were considered. Some Englishmen saw the opportunity to become planters and participate in the riches that West Indian planters had been displaying in England.

During the period of European conflict prior to 1756 the Caribbean colonies were often used as pawns, but the acquisition of colonies was clearly on their agenda. In the case of St. Vincent the fierce resistance of the indigenous people was a key factor in it being labelled a neutral island. The French and English clearly needed to come to an understanding and make certain concessions to each other if they were to take control of the islands not yet under their control. This they did at the Treaty of Paris. The British acted as though the right given to them in 1763 was one that could not be questioned, certainly, at least not by the indigenous people whom they regarded as being uncivilised. This is precisely why the struggles by the indigenous people were so significant, for clearly they were seen as objects, subjected to the dictates of the European powers who had no problem making decisions about their land without their involvement or consent.

Their focus was on the acquisition of virgin lands for the production of sugar. This intention was shown very early in the "Speech from the throne" in the British parliament, that paved the way for the establishment of Commissioners for the sale of the lands. By 1764 instructions were issued to the Commissioners, Sir William Young being head of the Commission. While they advertised the sale of lands and pointed to the possibilities of making fortunes on what they considered fertile lands, they recognised that they had to contend with the Garifuna who were settled on the best sugar lands. Their initial hope was that what they considered British humanity and generosity would endear that population to them (Young 19-20). They had hoped also, through these sales, to recover some of the costs involved in fighting their last war. The original instructions specified that no surveys were then to be taken of lands occupied and controlled by the "Black Caribs". They assumed the French had a great degree of influence over them but hoped that they could overcome that.

First governor of the conquered islands, General Robert Melville and his party undertook to tour St. Vincent, the Grenadines and Dominica and to be present at the sales of lands. Sales of lands in St. Vincent were initially slated for May 28, 1765. He encountered difficulties off Barrouallie because of strong currents. He took a barge and reached Ouashegunny, which we now know as Kingstown, at about noon where he was greeted by Lt. Governor Higginson, the Land Commissioners, and potential buyers of land from Antigua, Barbados and North America. Because of his late arrival, the beginning of the sale of lands was postponed to May 29. He was thus available for the start of the sale of lands that began with 'Town Lots'. Early sale of lands was very encouraging and in 1765 totalled over 7,000 acres, almost equalling total sales in Dominica and Tobago. Leases were also provided for French people who opted to remain on the island (From *Narrative of General Melville's Journey through the Islands*).

By 1767, 12,507 acres were sold, but this was largely on the Leeward side of the Island and represented most of the land there. That was the area occupied by some French small farmers and Kalinago people. The best sugar lands were on the Windward side, lands occupied by the indigenous people who were mainly Garinagu. The lands there were flatter and better watered and adequate to provide for the sugar mills, compared to the steeper Leeward areas. Prospective buyers who had come from some of the older sugar colonies and North America were very dissatisfied with their inability to acquire what they considered the best sugar lands anywhere, virgin as they considered them.

Fearing difficulty selling more lands and accommodating would-be planters willing to settle and invest in the sugar industry, the Commissioners very early began to build a case for the removal from the island of the indigenous people. They were described as savages who did little cultivation and whose presence would delay or restrict further sales. While they tried to convince the colonial authorities to have them removed, they hoped that in the interim they could get them to accept British sovereignty and the rights that were to come with it.

The French Abbé Valladares who had a working relationship with the indigenous people was used by the Land Commissioners as an intermediary to try to get them to acknowledge British sovereignty and its right to sell lands in their area. Abbé Valladares' report back to them offered little hope that they were prepared to accede to their request. This reinforced their efforts to get permission to have them removed either out of the island or possibly to Bequia, although they later recognised that the lack of rivers and a water supply would have been inhibiting factors there. They did not, of course, entertain any idea of settling them elsewhere on the mainland.

It was in 1768 after instructions were published in English and French that Abbé Valladares was given the responsibility of explaining the new instructions to them. It was during this visit that Chatoyer first came to our attention and makes his entrance to Vincentian history as a formidable defender of the country against British incursion. Valladares in his report describes his encounter at Grand Sable, "the principal settlement of the Caribs", with Chatoyer and a number of his men. Chatoyer, as spokesperson, questioned the authority of the King of England, with whom they had no acquaintance or knowledge. "Quel Roi", asked Chatoyer? Only the Governor of Martinique they were prepared to listen to. Valladares was told by others that Chatoyer spoke on their behalf.

It is not clear if at that time Chatoyer was as he was later acknowledged, "Paramount Chief". It appeared that the political structure of the Caribs involved different chiefs who were in charge of particular areas, but that in times of war, a "Paramount Chief" was selected. The French military officer, the Marquis de Lambertye, who had visited St. Vincent in the 1750s referred to one Touroüia, as the "sovereign cacique of the Black Caribs" of St. Vincent (See "French accounts of the Vincentian Caribs" by Peter Hulme in Joseph Palacio ed. *The Garifuna–A Nation Across Borders*). He might have been the predecessor to Chatoyer. How a paramount chief was selected is not known, but the view of some scholars is that he would have been selected based on expertise in war, although Lambertye stated that it was "a title passing from father to son since their arrival in America" (Palacio, p. 34). Taylor informs us that "An official British document of 1769 describes him as the 'Son of Legottes'". Does this, as Taylor seems to be implying, suggest that he was still a young person? In my work of 2002, I listed his age at time of death as between 55 and 58 years. In the 1773 treaty that ended the "First Carib War" Chatoyer was simply listed as one of 28 chiefs who signed the treaty with nothing to suggest that he was a paramount chief. In his first encounter with the British in 1768 he was described by Young as being at the head "of the mass of their people". Was he chief of the Grand Sable Caribs or was he then the paramount chief? There was some suggestion later that his area of control was on the northwestern side of the island. In the 1795 struggles he was said to have led his followers from the Leeward side with Duvalle heading those from the windward side. In any event the British and particularly Sir William Young at some point recognised him as a formidable figure and the prime Carib personality with whom they had to deal. The French also clearly recognised him as head of the Carib forces.

Young stated that Chatoyer, with some of his men, attended a Board of Commissioners meeting on June 14, 1768, and professed to be favourable to the terms. In reality there was nothing to suggest that they did, but the British later interpreted this to be a delaying tactic on their part, allowing them to gain time "and settle their plan of resistance" (Young, p. 39). In fact Young stated further, "Fatal experience had not yet taught that perfidy is the policy of the Charaib: that he is most submissive when he mediates revolt, most complacent when he designs outrage" (Young, 42). They might have been playing the English at their own game.

Efforts that continued to build a road were stopped at Colonaire (Calonery), the existing boundary separating English settlements and the area occupied by the Garifuna. Chatoyer again was at the head of his people from Grand Sable. The British officials in the colony along with the planters were of the view that any further attempts could only be made with military assistance.

In May 1769, an attempt was made by the British to continue the building of a road to the Charaib country. Members of the 32nd regiment who were part of the mission were confronted by the Caribs who surrounded them on the adjoining hills and cut off their communication, even preventing their access to water. Even when the remaining forces in the island came to their assistance, they were only allowed to leave when they agreed not to interfere in their area of the country and to discontinue attempts to build the road. The Land Commissioners response was to write to the Lords of Trade and Plantations in England, indicating to them that if the Caribs were allowed to remain where they were, their mission could never be accomplished. They pointed to the environment in which they functioned; one "surrounded with wood, makes any access to them, for the purpose of executing justice impracticable" (Young, p. 46-47, 52-54).

This was really a continuation of the case they had been building against the Black Caribs. In a letter of 1765, two years after occupying St. Vincent, the Commissioners spared no effort to point to them as obstacles to progress of the mission of the British. "They live in huts scattered in an irregular manner, at a great distance from each other, without any established subordination, claiming large tracts of wood land intervening, of which they make no use; and are besides possessed of other lands in the cleared parts of the country, which interfere much with the laying out plantations for sale…" (Young, p. 27).

In fact, as Fabel notes, even before British persons began occupying parts of St. Vincent, some officials, like Governors Stapleton of the Leeward Islands and Richard Dutton of Barbados, had been suggesting removal and even genocide for the indomitable indigenous people of St. Vincent (p. 142-143). In correspondence of 2 June 1762, Campbell Dalrymple, serving as temporary governor of Guadeloupe, informed Chief Minister the earl of Bute, that "St. Vincent is inhabited by numbers of the Caribbees, both black and swarthy (i.e., Yellow Caribs), so that nothing can be done there but by an expulsion or an extirpation of these inoffensive mortals" (Fabel, p 143-144).

On June 10, 1769, after coming from Grenada to St. Vincent, Lieutenant Governor Ulysses Fitzmaurice penned a letter to colonial secretary Hillsborough giving his assessment of the situation in the country. He was struck by the unease among the Garinagu, who feared not only of being deprived of their lands but also the possibility of being enslaved. He attributed this to French propaganda, pointing particularly at the French citizens who had left after the British takeover. He felt they harboured a grudge against the British and conveyed this hatred to the native people. This stood out for him because of the efforts made by the Crown and officials on the ground to make known to them "the king's most gracious and humane intentions to preserve them in their freedom, and to allow them good, proper, and sufficient lands for their support, maintenance and comfort" (Authentic Papers Relative to the Expedition Against the Charaibs and the Sale of Lands, p. 27).

He referred to their trade with the French in neighbouring territories that could easily supply their wants "which are easily satisfied". In his view the native inhabitants who lived on the border of British society were more civilised than those in the remote parts of the island. With reference to the recent Carib/British confrontation over the survey of lands and the attempt to build a road to facilitate their survey he emphasized the "Carib" declaration that they owed no sovereignty to any prince and that they were not subjects of the King of France who was in no position to cede their island to Britain. This was most likely a reference to the 1763 agreement that gave the British control of the colony. They reiterated that the whole Island belonged to them even though they had allowed the French access to parts of it, but they were determined to hold on to the rest.

The Lieutenant Governor emphasized a point which the Commissioners had been making, that without the admixture of "white inhabitants" they were likely to continue their fierce, "uncivilized, intractable, and lawless nature". Having estimated their fighting force at about 1,000 he felt that the presence of British troops and distribution of presents among them would have been enough to cause them to adhere to His Majesty's instructions without any bloodshed. Whatever expense was incurred was in his opinion likely to be recovered by the sale of their lands. In the meantime, he began the process of strengthening the island's defences.

The role of the West Indian lobby in England should not be underestimated. On January 22, 1770, they addressed a memorial on behalf of themselves and the planters in St. Vincent. Among the signers of that petition were Sir William Young and other planters from St. Vincent who were then in England and supported the use of a strong military force to ensure the continuation of the road (Fabel, 170). The planters from St. Vincent reiterated the idea of having them removed from the island (Young, p. 82).

A 1771 report from the Land Commissioners de-emphasized the issue of land and stressed their defiance of the crown. "the honour of the crown now becomes concerned for the protection of its subjects, against a race of lawless people, who when prompted by liquor or ill designing persons, may commit any violence without being subject to control" (Young 78-79). They argued for continuing to build a road through the lands they held but with a strong military force and "allotting them lands for their ample subsistence". The Commissioners' report was supported by a memorial of the Council and Assembly that described the resisting Garifuna as "artful and daring…who had shaken every principle which the commissioners had laboured to establish for attaching the Charaibs as a people to the crown of Great Britain" (Young 80-81).

Colonial Secretary, Lord Hillsborough finally decided to accede to their wishes and began to put things in place. Sir William Young who was then lieutenant governor of Dominica was given the authority to head a committee dealing with the situation in St. Vincent. British army forces stationed in North America and in St. Kitts, Antigua, Dominica, and Nassau were to assemble in St. Vincent. There was, however, some delay because of hurricanes affecting some of the islands. There was also the necessity to build temporary barracks for the soldiers since there were not enough buildings in Kingstown to house them. The number of military personnel who eventually assembled in St. Vincent was 2, 275 (Fabel, p. 196). These were to be accompanied by the island militia and slaves if needed.

Information on the 1772-1773 war used here was to some extent influenced by the work of Michael Craton, Barnard Marshall, and Robin Fabel who, more than others were able to access correspondence, both official and private, between St. Vincent and Britain and American and British newspapers of that time.

The total number of forces did not arrive before the end of August, but some activity was already in progress. Frigates were already in place to monitor and prevent any communication with the French islands. The British consulted the governor of Martinique urging him not to assist the Garifuna, which he agreed to, but with the reservation that it was going to be difficult to prevent private traders. As will be shown later, trade with the French had been important in the life of the indigenous people.

The order issued to Young had been made in April but did not reach him until June, shortly after which he journeyed to St. Vincent. There seemed to have been some ambiguity regarding the executing authority for the war effort. Despite the communication sent to Young, Colonel William Dalrymple was given the responsibility to take charge of the St. Vincent campaign. Governor Leyborne would also have assumed that he had major responsibility. Even though the order for the St. Vincent campaign was given in April 1772, operations did not begin until September. This meant having to contend with the hurricane and rainy season.

Contrary to the beliefs of the Council, Assembly and planters, the large force assembled in St. Vincent did not produce the kind of effect on the Garifuna that they had hoped. The Garinagu attacked targets in different parts of the country, including Marriaqua in St. George's Parish and the Cumberland Valley in St. Patrick. Fabel notes that among the Garifuna party were Kalinagos, which surprised the British given the view commonly held that they were not a part of the struggle.

A local force was assembled, made up of slaves, French small planters, free blacks, and free mulatto volunteers whose training and mission was to have them operate in the woods. This had later to be called off since they seemed reluctant to undertake that task. It is of note that William Young did not deal with the details of the military operations but concluded that the operations were prolonged because of "the humane and cautious system on which the campaign was conducted". He did, however, refer to the British establishment of military posts, some around the coast that might have finally prompted the Garinagu's willingness to negotiate terms that finally brought the war to an end.

Gun Powder Magazine- restored in 2017 by the Owia Heritage Organisation. This was originally built in 1773 as part of the British Military works.

But there was much more involved. The military strategy of the Garifuna was a key factor. Their use of what we today will consider guerrilla tactics, avoiding direct confrontation but employing hit and run tactics, availing themselves of the woods, with which they were intensely familiar, using ambush, digging trenches, and attacking in small groups. When attacked by British soldiers they burnt their huts and provision grounds and retreated further into the woods. The British would have preferred to deal with stationary attacks where their superior military weaponry would have been advantageous. They resented their failure to stand and fight. Those tactics not only frustrated them but stalled the progress and reduced the effectiveness of British military superiority. One report that was brought to parliament's attention noted that "...the woods are so thick that they knock our men down with the greatest security to themselves, as it is impossible to see them" (Fabel, p. 186).

A major factor was the tropical weather conditions at that time of the year. Sickness and death affected the soldiers and their families, some of them having been allowed to take their families along. Letters home from soldiers complained about sickness and death and the low morale that resulted. In parliament there were reports of the number of sick soldiers; in November 1772, 220 soldiers were reported sick. A letter from Governor Leyborne to the Colonial Secretary in October 1772 stated, "I flatter myself, we shall soon be able to give your lordship some satisfactory account of our proceedings, tho' I must confess the conduct of the Charibbs is more serious and formidable and I see greater difficultys (sic) in the execution of His Majesty's Commands than I expected. I very much fear that their reduction will be a work of time, for they possess a country very inaccessible and seem to have a knowledge how to avail themselves of this advantage" (Marshall, 2007, p. 14).

Major operations took place at Grand Sable as the British were able to move substantial numbers of soldiers there. Although affected by the tides and Garifuna attacks, this turned out to be critical to the final outcome. The British had been able to establish posts, many of them around the coast. This affected the Garifuna's trade with the French islands, with many of their provision grounds burnt not only by themselves in their hit and run retreats, but also by slaves engaged by the British to do that task. Of great importance was the impact it had on their ability to fish, which was one of their major sources of food. This access to food and fish played a critical part in the decisions they later made. Additionally, as they got into the early months of 1773 the change of weather suited the British but low morale and frustration still remained.

The fact that the efforts to control the Garifuna and get them to accept the conditions the British were prepared to offer them went on much longer than was expected, generated some interest in England. Private letters sent back to England and official ones as the one of October 1772 from governor Leyborne to the colonial secretary painted a picture that was not very optimistic and indicated that the struggle might be much longer than expected.

Opponents of the Lord North administration in England used the concerns about what was happening in St. Vincent to criticise the administration. One letter in Scots magazine written by Probus, obviously a pseudonym, accused the government of reviving the Spanish cruelties as witnessed in the conquest of Mexico for the benefit of "avaricious merchants, landholders and venal commissioners" (Marshall, 2007, p. 22-23). This added to reports of widespread sickness among soldiers and their families, of deaths and harsh weather conditions that created a low morale among soldiers.

An officer from a Royal Navy vessel in Kingstown also had his say in a letter home in November 1772; "...I reckon very few of the planters will survive the campaign. I am afraid they too justly deserve their fate, as the expedition was set on foot at their instigation to serve mercenary purposes conceived between them and the merchants they correspond with in London. This expedition, little as you may think it, will cost Great Britain about one million pounds sterling, besides the lives that will be lost, as well as the infamy it will bring upon the national character to butcher a parcel of innocent savages in cold blood" (Fabel, p. 183).

Granville Sharpe better known for his success in the James Somerset case that he argued before Judge Mansfield in 1772 and his role in the Abolition movement seemed, according to Robin Fabel, to have been in communication with the Colonial Secretary and to have brought his 'moral influence' to bear on the issue. This period was also one that featured in parliament issues related to the American colonies and India. Eventually Cabinet seemed to have taken a decision to bring the contentious issue in St. Vincent to an end and the Colonial Secretary had written to Governor Leyborne on December 9 conveying the wishes of Cabinet. The debate, however, continued in parliament and an inquiry demanded by opponents of the administration concluded in February that the expedition was "unjust and inhumane".

But unknown to those in England, conditions in St. Vincent led the parties to agree on a treaty. Contrary to the impression conveyed by William Young and Charles Shepherd, the agreement to bring the matter to an end with a peace treaty was in the interest of both parties. Although the British soldiers achieved some measure of success at Grand Sable with the large number of soldiers they were able to land there, they had not been able to penetrate much further. Their low morale continued, and sickness and death took their toll. Later, the governor was able to inform the Colonial Secretary that about 72 men were killed, 428 sick and another 110 died from disease.

Alexander Anderson who became Director of the Botanical Garden in 1784 when Britain resumed control of St. Vincent, was in touch with eyewitnesses and participants of the War. His comments therefore are important. About the end of the war and the treaty of 1773, he stated, "They fought with great courage and resolution, at least obliging a formidable army of regular troops to a cessation of hostilities. We were obliged to give them their terms" (p. 53). He argued that the war was too expensive and destructive and noted that the Officers were affected by the climate "and with savages whom they could never bring to action (in) this mode of warfare unknown. The poisoned arrow flew from the thicket! The object of its vengeance know not the quarters from whence it came" (p. 48-49).

The Garifuna also welcomed and might finally, after initially failing to respond to overtures at peace, have taken the initiative and signalled their intent to end the struggle and to work out the necessary terms. The ability of the British to construct posts on the coast in a number of areas created hardships for them and the presence of naval ships obstructed their important trade with the French islands. The British, however, never knew how many armed men they had to confront.

Anderson, quoting eyewitnesses that were privy to the transactions made the point that when orders for peace came from England, they were already laying down their arms. It has to be noted that the treaty was negotiated and agreed to on February 17 before the arrival of the December 9 correspondence from Colonial Secretary Dartmouth. In looking at correspondence between the colonies and England during this time one has to consider the length of time it took to exchange correspondence between Britain and its colonies. Dalrymple and Governor Leyborne, to the extent that he might have been involved in those negotiations, would have borne in mind the positions that had previously been taken by the Colonial Office and would also have been aware of the debates in parliament. It was thus not only in the interest of both parties but also of the Lord North administration, given the parliamentary conclusion that expressed criticism of the war.

Prior to the war the British had been quite unfamiliar with the territory of the Garifuna, having made only minor incursions that were stopped by Chatoyer and his men. Given the tactics of the Garifuna the circumstances and conditions under which the battle was fought had not changed significantly. The British forces were also shocked by their strategies and their ability to have held out for so long. It is, of course, not known how many of the Garinagu were killed, although it is likely that the numbers were less than those of the British. They were also clearly ignorant of the commander of their forces that had created so many difficulties for them. Valentine Morris who succeeded Leyborne suggested that the leader and strategist might have been Jean Baptiste but there is all indication that the man who led the charge and was the chief strategist was Chatoyer. Governor Leyborne had even indicated to the Colonial Secretary that Chatoyer was referred to by his men as general (Fabel, 193).

The 1773 Treaty which sought to have the Garifuna and Kalinago people recognise the British Crown as their sovereign and hopefully end the tensions turned out not to be so. The planters, in any event, were dissatisfied with the terms of the treaty. The treaty certainly did not change the determination of the indigenous people not to surrender their lands. It was no more than a "holding point". This is discussed further in the next chapter.

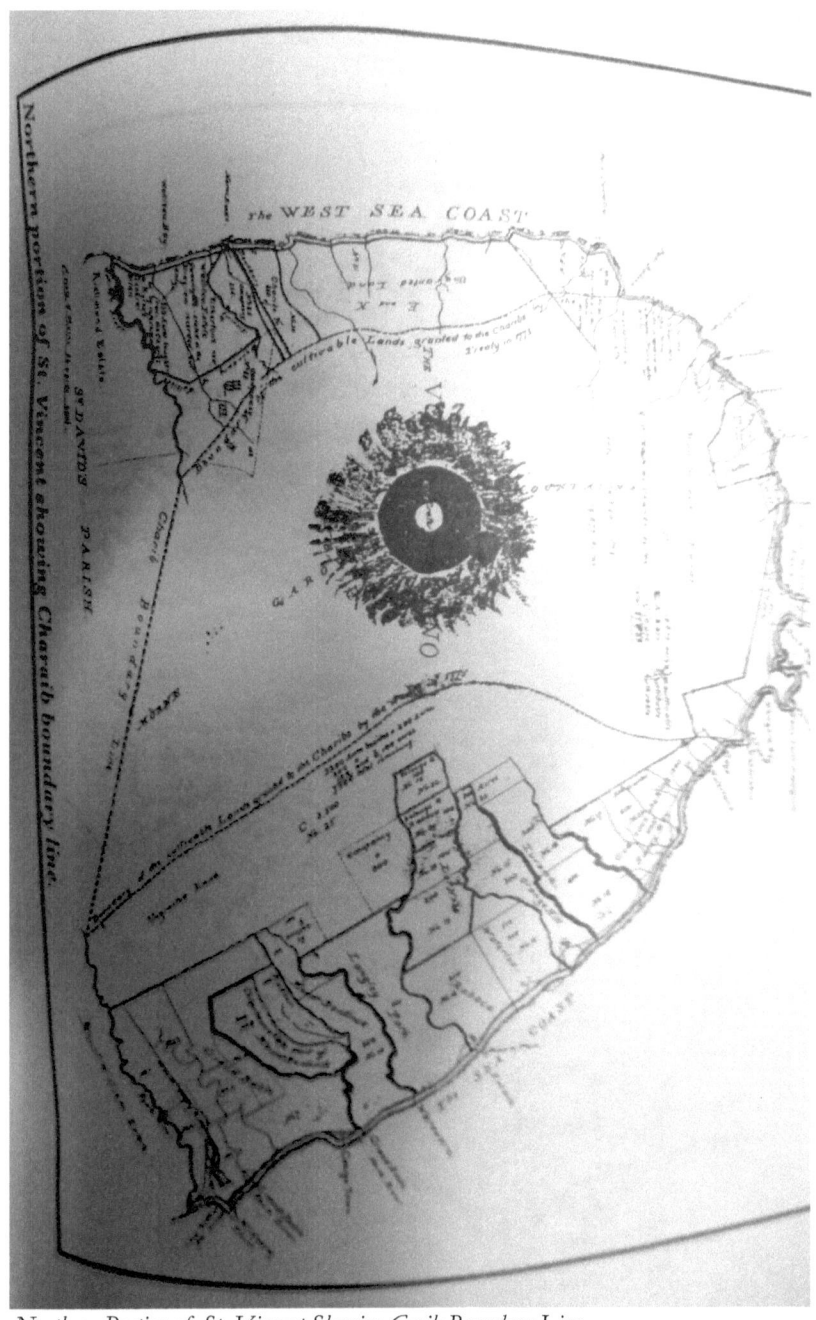

Northern Portion of St. Vincent Showing Carib Boundary Line

Chapter 4
From Treaty to War

The Garifuna, after earlier rejecting an offer to negotiate, finally agreed to end the war and begin negotiating a treaty. As was stated earlier, it was in the interest of both parties to do so. It is difficult to speak about clear winners. Some historians, including Marshall and Craton, even described it as a stalemate, Craton in fact, called it an agreement with "equal parties, though it was predictably full of loaded clauses" (p. 151). One can look at the issue of land. As will be seen shortly, the Garifuna retained most of their lands. This is significant given the fact that access to those prized lands was what created the tensions that eventually led to war. The planters were certainly not happy with the resolution of the land issue. We have to note that sugar production in the other ceded islands was increasing significantly. St. Vincent's production also increased but largely through use of lands on the west coast that were sold by French landholders who had opted to leave.

Robin Fabel went a step further and stated that there was a sense in which they won the war without the battle. He argued that "they had created a situation in which British investors lost interest in acquiring land anywhere in St. Vincent, least of all in those parts of it immediately adjacent to the Carib country". This is perhaps a case of over stretching one's point for although many of the planters and would be planters became frustrated and lost interest, when the British eventually acquired the lands there was no shortage of persons wanting to buy them. Actually, some of them began to encroach on the lands even before the Government had sorted out some legal technicalities surrounding a grant of 6,000 acres given to Thomas Browne who had fought in the American War.

The Treaty of February 17, 1773, was signed by Colonel William Dalrymple on behalf of the British Government and by twenty-eight Caribs, most of them presumably chiefs, among them Chatoyer, Jean Baptiste and Duvallée.

Clause IV of the Treaty dealt with the issue of lands. There were differences by commentators about the original boundary lines. Kirby and Martin had described the boundary line, allegedly drawn up by the French that divided the country between the Garifuna and Kalinago peoples, as being in the vicinity of Colonarie. But they later referred to the 1773 Treaty as having shifted the boundary from Stubbs to Byrea. Barnard Marshall, however, states that the boundaries of lands allotted to the Garifuna were shifted from the River Colonaire to River Byrea on the Eastern side of the Island, some 2,000 acres (Marshall, *Slavery, Law and Society*, p. 26). Taylor, gave a slightly higher figure, estimating land transferred to the Crown as 4,000 acres, instead of the 10,000 acres that would have been involved in the shift from Stubbs to Byrea. In any event, the bulk of the land that the planters had hoped for and which prompted the wars was left in the hands of the Garifuna, lands the planters held in high regard, considering them virgin and fertile. The Garifuna on the other hand, were expected to acknowledge and take an oath of loyalty to the King who was to be seen and accepted as the 'rightful' sovereign of the island. They were to accept and submit themselves to the Crown's laws. This, however, applied to their relations and transactions with British subjects and did not apply to their customs and relationships within the area over which they retained control.

One other issue that had been of great concern to the British and featured previously in agreements with the Kalinago and Garifuna people was the return of runaway slaves. Père Labat, on his visit to St. Vincent on September 24, 1700, indicated that the "Caribs" had formerly returned runaways to their masters or sold them to the French and Spaniards, but stopped doing that and accepted them as part of their community (Labat, p. 137). Clause viii stated that any runaway slaves in their possession were to be handed over to them, and they were urged not to encourage or shelter any other, the punishment being forfeiture of lands and exile. Another clause stated that any deserters from the British service and runaway slaves from the French were also to be delivered to them. The treaty gave the right to persons authorised by the Governor to be entitled to enter Carib territory in pursuit or in search of expected deserters or runaways.

The issue of runaways was always going to be a problem because the Kalinagos had even before the 18th century been encouraging the settlement of runaways into their ranks. Governor Valentine Morris had considered runaways his biggest problem and in 1777, four years after the treaty, decided to become personally involved in recapturing runaways. He claimed to have achieved some success through negotiations with "Carib" chiefs. His efforts, however, failed to achieve the success he might have hoped. The "Caribs", like the English, despite what Young had been trying to convey, saw the 1773 treaty as a temporary holding measure. The "Garifuna" who had been formed from a union between the Kalinago and escaped slaves realised that in any future encounter with the British the runaways were going to be an important force.

There was to be no "undue" intercourse with the French. They were prepared to facilitate the sale of their produce and trade with other British islands. No strangers were to be permitted to settle in their quarters without permission from the authorities. When called on to attend the Governor, "Carib chiefs" or any others were expected to comply. They were to assist the British against their enemies. Additionally, strangers or white persons were not allowed to settle among them without permission, clearly geared to their relationship with the French. Any members of their community who wanted to leave the country were to be assisted in doing so. Of importance, too, was that any of their community who objected to and refused to accept the agreement was to be considered "enemies of both parties, and the most effectual means used to reduce them".

The "Caribs" long standing relationship with the French was not going to be easily displaced by a treaty that the "Caribs" obviously did not take seriously. It was a holding point for them as it probably was for the British. The French were of the view that the Carib hatred of the British was sucked in "with their mother's milk" and had become "a national prejudice" (quoted by Taylor, p. 100). Anderson described the Carib trade with the English as trifling compared to what they had with the French. He claimed that at that time "Seldom any of their chiefs or principal men came to Kingstown, to such a height had their aversion to the English become" (p. 57).

It is interesting that one of the clauses aimed to prevent "undue" intercourse with the French islands. What exactly did that mean? One would assume that this would have aimed at preventing trade in weaponry and where other trade was concerned would not have applied in times when both countries were at peace. Among the items of trade with the French were hammocks, baskets and tobacco. In exchange they got not only weaponry-muskets, ammunition and sabers, but also metal objects, cutlasses, wine, and rum.

Was the treaty likely to ensure peace and facilitate amicable relations between both parties? Clearly tensions were bound to remain. The treaty did not satisfy the interests of the planters. The indigenous people on the other hand had vowed never to surrender their lands and would obviously have been on the watch for any further efforts to take more or all of their land. The fear that was previously expressed by the Commissioners and planters about the difficulty of living with the Caribs in the same island would not have disappeared. How some areas of the treaty were to be monitored was certainly debatable.

They swore "in the name of the immortal God, and Christ Jesus" and pledged "true allegiance to his Majesty George the Third, of Great Britain, France, and Ireland...." What all of that meant in reality is questionable, for the religious groups, including French Catholic missionaries and later the Methodists, had not been very successful in converting the native people to Christianity. As to pledging allegiance to the king, we must remember that in events leading up to the war they expressed no interest in having an allegiance to a king about whom they knew little. "Quel roi" asked Chatoyer? Would the treaty have changed this?

As stated before, the treaty mainly held things in abeyance. The issue of relationship with the French islands would not have been easily resolved. The Garifuna and Kalinagos before them had greater trust in their relationship with the French, who did not then represent a threat to their land. They said earlier that they were prepared to relate and take advice from the French, but stated unapologetically that they were equally prepared to deny them access to the land that they controlled. In fact, they were critical of the 1763 Peace Treaty since the French did not have the authority to turn over their lands to the British. In the scheme of things, as seen by the British and French, this was a matter between "civilised" nations. The geopolitics of that time, which the Garifuna clearly understood, would have determined how they related to both countries.

One suspects that the earlier willingness of the Kalinago to allow the French to settle among them would have been influenced by geopolitical considerations. The French, moreover, were prepared to go into small farming that did not create any strong desire for Kalinago land. They had certainly earlier harboured that desire, but had come to accept the reality, even if temporarily. The native people also understood, particularly in the 17th and early 18th centuries, that the French and British were constantly at war and that the French were prepared to provide them with assistance as part of their struggles with the British. In the 1772 war the British were able to get the French to deny assistance to the Garifuna, but the position taken, and future relationships, would have depended on British–French relations at the time.

The Methodists attempt to work with the indigenous people bore little fruit. They were actually suspicious of their role, Thomas Coke suggesting this was because of French influence. The British were constantly overplaying the degree of influence the French had over the Garifuna. They clearly were about protecting themselves and defending their land. Their attack on the Abbe Valdares, despite his earlier close relationship with them, was based on their feeling that he had been double crossing them with the English. Long before this, the massacre of two Jesuit priests in 1654 by the Kalinagos was an effort to exact retribution from the French for injustices they felt had been committed against them. They had expressed on different occasions their close relationship with the French, but were of the view that in the end it was their interest that mattered. The Methodist Baxter and his wife, who had been living in the boundary area of the Carib territory hoping to get converts, were aware of their hostile attitude to them and eventually left and returned to Kingstown.

The hollowness of the treaty was shown with Garifuna support for the French in their attack on St. Vincent in 1779. William Young and Charles Shephard were quick to blame them. Shephard argued that the planters adopted a different attitude to them after the 1773 treaty, "endeavouring by a constant and uniform civility to make them friends, and to conciliate their esteem" (p. 36). The question posed by Shephard's comment is, what was the alternative? The British government was not going to quickly get into another war after the experience of 1772 and the storm it created in parliament. As can be seen, too, from Commissioner Young's earlier comments, the attitude adopted by the colonials was to hope to win over the "Caribs" by professing good treatment and allowing them to be subjects of the king, entitled to the rights of British subjects. He referred to what he described as "Christian mercy and British benevolence". They had previously on different occasions intimated to the home government the impossibility of living with them. The 1772 war would clearly have strengthened that view. The Garinagu understood this and in any event had no wish to be British or for that matter French citizens. What resulted therefore was a waiting game by both parties. Young indicated that in the five years after the Treaty there was no disturbance and that their main intercourse with the Garifuna was at the Kingstown markets where they took their produce for sale. He regarded this as proof of their domestication and recognition of themselves as British subjects.

On different occasions, however, Chatoyer and representatives met with the governor concerning rumours of plans to make them slaves. The tensions remained, creating almost a state of "cold war". The year 1778, two years after Morris's frantic search for runaway slaves, brought the tensions to a climax. France entered the War of American Independence, supporting the rebelling colonists, and began activities in the Caribbean that included an attack on St. Vincent. They sought the assistance of the Garifuna who seemed quite willing to do so. Chatoyer's carbet was their strategy-planning venue. Communications with the French in Martinique which had been forbidden without British agreement, was stepped up with ammunition being part of that trade. It would appear anyhow that the trade with the French had never really stopped after 1773.

The British arrest of a French officer working with the Garifuna met with a stern response from Chatoyer, warning them that any other attempt to repeat such action would have been to the detriment of the British, even suggesting to them that none of their soldiers would have lived to tell the tale (Taylor, p. 88). The Governor continued to remind them of their pledge of loyalty to the British which came with the 1773 treaty, but that obviously meant little to the Garifuna, to whom the Treaty, as Craton suggested, was a "temporary expedient". The fighting forces they assembled with French training were critical to the outcome of the war and the surrender of the British. Chatoyer's role was emphasized by the fact that he was a part of the negotiating team that agreed on the terms that were built into the 1779 peace agreement. The French installed a governor when St. Vincent passed into their hands. They, however, made no major attempt to bring about any changes, suggesting perhaps that they expected the colony to be returned to the British following the war. It should be noted that there was a failed attempt by the British in 1780 to recapture St. Vincent.

There were, however, some tensions between the Garinagu and French, attributed largely to the governor who was put in charge, Monsieur Dumontel. They even sent a letter to the governor in Martinique who was able to calm the tensions.

The Treaty of Paris in 1783, following the end of the War of American Independence, placed St. Vincent once more into the hands of the British. Some British commentators, in light of later developments, played up what they considered efforts to work along with and accept the Garifuna and Kalinago communities and to extend friendship and provide to them access to British justice and goodwill. Bryan Edwards, who admitted having to change some of his views after reading Young's account of the Black Caribs, stated that despite Carib misconduct that led to the 1779 war, the British made no effort to exact revenge and took no advantage of them when they resumed control of St. Vincent in 1784. They were allowed to return to their possessions. Sir William Young claimed they were treated "as an ignorant and deluded people, whose conduct needed compassion rather than pardon; and who were to be acquitted (as by a jury on insanity) in humane consideration of weakness and of folly" (Young, p. 104).

After the 1773 Treaty, according to Alexander Anderson, many of the Garinagu never moved beyond the Byrea boundary. Some of them had even moved back into areas supposed to have been put under British control. Most were eventually forced out by English planters who, after 1773, were converting cotton lands into sugar plantations. Anderson was critical of that, suggesting they could have been allowed to reap their crops and some even given small lots. That might, in his view, have detached them from the other Garifuna people, citing the assistance some were able to give to the planters in that area in getting their produce to the ships waiting outside. He admitted, however, that some who remained, later joined the fight against the British.

What is significant is that sugar cultivation was on the increase because of the establishment of additional sugar works in areas the Garifuna surrendered by the terms of the 1773 treaty. As indicated earlier, some Loyalists who had fought for the British in the American War of Independence and planters from colonies that had long been in sugar production, were still actively seeking lands and an opportunity to get into sugar production, especially on new lands not exhausted as those of the older sugar producing colonies. Some were at least occupying, even though in small quantities, parts of the prized sugar lands. On his visit to St. Vincent in 1791 Sir William Young (junior) had indicated that the lands around the Byrea boundary line had risen in value "and every settler is growing rich" (*Wild Majesty*, p. 214). With the help of those Caribs who had remained in the Byrea area they were able to have their sugar taken out and supplies brought in from sloops that were forced to remain some distance away because of the rough seas on that eastern part of the island.

William Young whose book on the "Black Caribs" has strongly influenced the story of their encounter with the British, played up the relationship of Chatoyer with his father, stating that the elder Young and other planters went out of their way to cultivate their friendship and spread good will among them. He stated that Chatoyer, Duvallée and their sons and other chiefs were often guests at his house and the Villa estate, receiving "the most flattering attentions and hospitality from the gentleman and his family…. The beautiful garden island near Calliaqua, called Young Island, with a convenient villa built on it, was by the proprietor allowed for the Charaibs to refresh, or sleep upon, going to, or returning from Kingstown and occasionally as a station for their fisheries" (p. 107).

"Young Island" today, is the site of a hotel. Kirby and Martin, in their work on the Black Caribs, referred to a legend that suggested that Young Island was given to Sir William Young in exchange for two horses that were admired by Chatoyer (Caracas 1985, p. 46). Traditional ownership of Carib lands was communal and not individual, and so the lands were not Chatoyer's to give, especially in a period of peace when the 'paramount' chief's power was supposed to have been reduced. This traditional adherence to communal lands was even cited in 1902 during a holding phase in the eruption of the Soufriere volcano when, in a petition from the Caribs of Morne Ronde, seeking land to replace that destroyed by the eruption, they referred to their communal ownership of lands.

Two sons of Chatoyer were said to have been living with a family, presumably British, that wanted to take them to Europe but was unable to do so since Chatoyer was not around to give his consent. Another son who went by the name of John Dimmey was being tutored by the Methodist missionary Baxter (Taylor p. 110, from Thomas Coke, p. 262-3). To continue to make the point that the British were harbouring good relationships with the Caribs, references were made to the Carib women taking their vegetable and poultry to the Kingstown market. Chatoyer and Duvallée were said to have owned estates on which they presumably planted cotton and owned slaves, having obtained loans and sureties from British gentlemen, "and each of them by these means had purchased slaves, and was comparatively rich" (p. 106-107). Young argues that "Money civilizes in the first instance...as it corrupts in the last; the savage labouring for himself, soon ceases to be a savage; the slave to money becomes a subject to government and he becomes a useful subject" (p. 214, *Wild Majesty*, "William Young's Tour of the Islands").

Since 1764, when the Land Commissioners arrived in the colony, they had hoped to convince the Garinagu to accept and participate in aspects of British life, but nothing since then would have led them to believe that they were willing to accept that. The war of 1772-1773 and that of 1779, when the colony was taken over by the French with the help of the Garifuna, would have made them even more distrustful of the Garifuna people. It was, as stated before, a waiting game since the English's original and continuing aim was to take control of the lands of the indigenous people.

British planters were generally not prepared to have any competition from the colonial peoples with anything they were producing, even recognising that many of their people who had been planting cotton were now turning to sugar. Encouraging Chatoyer and Duvallée to get into cotton production appears quite far-fetched. How was it possible for them to be using slaves on their "plantations" when it was part of the strategy of the Garifuna to attract and encourage slaves to escape and become part of their community? Did their so-called slaves join them in war against the British? To whom were they selling their cotton and what was the process involved? With the British planters continuing greed for more land, why were they assisting Chatoyer and Duvallé in getting plantations and getting into European-type agriculture?

Sir William Young, junior, who had inherited his father's properties in St. Vincent, visited the colony in 1791 and in his journal of that tour referred to persons travelling near to the areas occupied by the Garifuna who looked over "the delightful plains of Grand Sable from Mount Young and exclaimed 'What a pity this country yet belongs to the savage Charaibes'". He indicated that it had "awakened jealousies and apprehensions, and some French discontented fugitives from Martinico and elsewhere had (as had been heard from the Charaibes at Kingston) (sic) given a rumour that I was come out with some project for dispossessing them by the English government" (p. 211).

The suspicions and tensions that had perhaps intensified since the first Carib War remained with both parties. The British, very sensitive to this and very much aware of the mistrust of the Garifuna people, were continuing to pay attention to their defences, and a new fortification was being organised at Berkshire Hill where Fort Charlotte was to be located. It isn't clear, precisely, when the construction of the fort started, even though it appeared to before the war of 1795, but one of the things that stands out about it is that the cannons and the holders for the cannons were pointing inwards, not to enemies outside but to their more formidable enemies inland, the Garifuna and their French allies. The British, meanwhile, did not indicate an abandonment of their desire to take control of the lands of the indigenous people, despite comments left for posterity by their countrymen.

The tensions and suspicions had grown remarkably. The final showdown that led to the death of paramount chief Chatoyer, the exile of the majority of Garifuna people, and British control of their lands, came in 1795. They had long since argued that the Garifuna control of prized lands was an obstacle to the expansion of their sugar industry. The movement for the abolition of the slave trade had already started in England, but there was nothing to indicate to them at that time that it had any chance of success. Their planting lobby in England had so far succeeded in protecting their interests. It was important to them to develop the sugar industry and that was their main focus. The tensions were increasing and the geopolitical climate sharpening with the outbreak of the French Revolution and its impact not only in Europe, but also in the Caribbean. The next chapter explores this further.

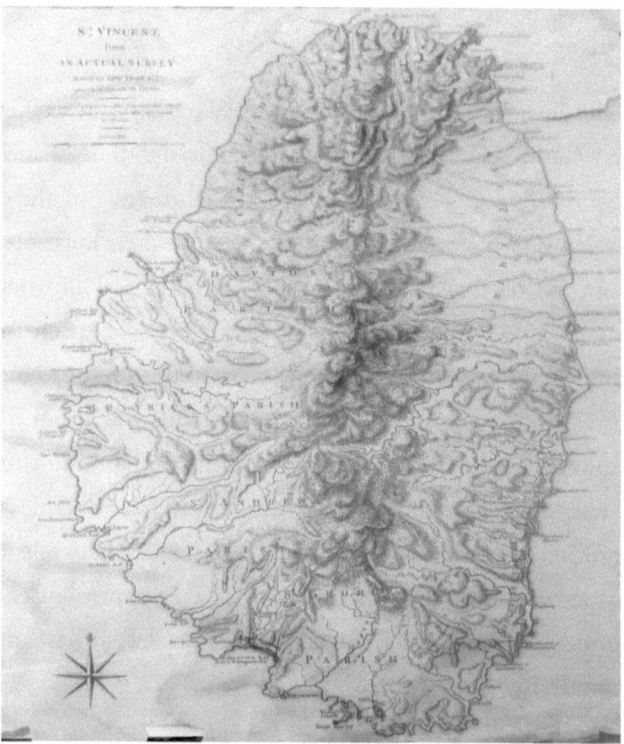

St. Vincent Actual Survey in 1733

Chapter 5
THE FINAL SHOWDOWN
The Death of Chatoyer
and Exile of the Garifuna

An examination of what was written about the 2nd Carib War and the decision to exile the "Caribs" from St. Vincent, made it obvious that the intention of those who wrote about the war was to single out the "Caribs" as the culprits who pushed the British to take the action they did, after having made every attempt, they argued, to accommodate and live with them. They believed the Treaty of Paris of 1763 gave them rights to the lands in St. Vincent. The Garinagu who were the ones objecting to their presence and were leading the struggle against them, had, in their view, illegally seized control of lands that belonged to the Kalinago people.

As was indicated before, geopolitical considerations had been key factors in the indigenous people's struggle against the British, who treated them as objects rather than people who had control over their own lives. European civilisation was what mattered to the British, so the decision to divide the Caribbean colonies between themselves and the French should not have been questioned. In 1772 the British had been assured by the French that they were not going to offer any assistance to the Garifuna.

The view was often expressed by the British that the indigenous people had merely been doing the bidding of the French and that most of the problems came about because of French influence. It needs to be repeated here that the Garifuna, like the Kalinagos before them, had simply been responding to, and making their own calculations in addressing, the situation that confronted them. They had understood the nature of the relationship between the British and French and were prepared to use differences between them to further their own interests. They were, at the same time, more inclined to accept aid from the French with whom they had a closer relationship.

Wars in the latter part of the 17th and in the 18th century between the British and French, even when they were driven by European concerns and issues, usually played themselves out in the colonies, as one can see from the frequent transfer of colonies following those wars. The sugar trade had been very important to the British and French and so acquisition of colonies to further the sugar trade was always a consideration for them.

The French Revolution of 1789 had repercussions in the colonies. In France's most important colony of St. Domingue, the divisions that appeared in France were replicated and provided an opportunity at first for the Mulattoes to seek the rights they felt they were denied. With divisions taking place in St. Domingue and the French concentrating on their domestic situation, the slaves used the occasion to push for their freedom. The British later joined the European coalition against France and their rivalry over control of the sugar colonies resulted in the war being extended to the colonies. The British seizure of the colonies of Martinique and Guadeloupe in 1794 and their earlier entry into St. Domingue, led the National

Convention Government in France to send one of its emissaries, Victor Hugues, to try to retake their colonies and to stir up revolt among dissatisfied groups, which included French planters who had been residing in some of the British colonies.

Hugues had established contact with the Garifuna in St. Vincent who had their grievances with the British and welcomed French assistance in their efforts to reassert full control of their land. The French Revolution's cry of liberty and equality and their abolition of slavery in 1794 would have warmed the hearts of slaves in colonies like Grenada and the Garifuna in St. Vincent. He pledged French help to Chatoyer and his people with French soldiers and arms and ammunition. Through the coordination of Hugues, French-speaking coffee planters and small holders, led by coloured coffee planter Julien Fedon, were to lead the rebellion starting in Grenada on March 10, 1795. The Grenada uprising, however, started on March 1, and Governor Seton of St. Vincent received news of the revolt on March 5. He immediately put his militia under arms. It was to be split into groups defending the plantations, with others stationed at Berkshire Hill to overlook the town and small British forces stationed in the colony were to be used to protect the boundaries that divided British residents from the lands occupied by the "Caribs". Although a British planter, William Greig reported that he was warned by a "Carib" that an attack was imminent, other indigenous people whom British personnel had been sent to contact professed no knowledge of such intention and proceeded to relate to them in their accustomed way. When the governor, however, invited Chatoyer and other "Carib" chiefs to a meeting, Chatoyer's answer, it was reported, was that it was too late for such a meeting.

By March 8, 1795, the situation had changed dramatically with an attack by Garifuna forces on an estate belonging to a French lady, Madame La Croix, at Evesham who had a close relationship with the British. Militia forces sent to investigate the situation were able to arrest a small number of Garifuna men, the others having escaped. Even then there were no compelling signs there was going to be any major attack, but the following day, March 9, the militia forces in the north Windward area sought military aid since word had been received that a Garifuna attack in that area was underway. On March 10, news was received that a number of estates were already being attacked and burnt. In the area of Massarica river, now known as South Union, their men came under attack from Garifuna forces on a surrounding ridge with others in the rear that used the cover of the cane fields and a silk cotton tree that had been cut down. The British forces were left with no alternative but to retreat to Kingstown, with 31 of their men losing their lives. Shephard described their retreat as "precipitate and disorderly", a manner that created panic among English residents in that area of the country, who abandoned everything and hastened to Kingstown for protection.

Governor Seton issued a proclamation describing what he considered a "cruel and unprovoked attack...aggravated by every circumstance of savage Barbarity". He declared the attack as being led by Chatoyer, who was "acknowledged by them as General and Commander of the whole" and referred to the oaths of allegiance they had taken to the King in 1773. He noted they were aided by a lawless Banditti of French inhabitants. He considered the attack as a treasonable plot whose intention was to exterminate the English inhabitants. He was not prepared to apply the laws of war, except for those who were prepared to surrender before March 25, and who would not have been involved or participants in the rebellion

(BA: CO 260/13 XC/ A/ 63011). All blame for what was called the 2nd Carib War was to be placed on the Garifuna people, whom they claimed failed to live up to obligations undertaken with the signing of the 1773 treaty.

The Garifuna attack from the north windward area was led by Duvallée whose forces destroyed sugar works and cane fields on their way to Kingstown. He reached Dorsetshire Hill on the morning of Thursday, March 12, and took control of the fort, pulling down the British flag and hoisting that of the French Republic. Chatoyer led forces from the Leeward end where he was joined by French settlers, some of whom, Kirby and Martin claimed, said they were forced to do so under duress. Chatoyer moved outside of Kingstown and joined forces with Duvallée on March 12. They succeeded in dragging, from the Stubbs battery, a "twelve and four pounder" weighing about 3,000 pounds, to Dorsetshire Hill about 12 miles away.

British Attack and the Death of Chatoyer

Canon at Fort Charlotte

Governor Seton moved with his valuable documents to the fort at Berkshire Hill and concerned himself with the security of the town, placing militia forces there and at adjoining estates; sugar cane fields in some areas were burnt to prevent their use as cover by the Garifuna. A British post was established at Sion Hill as part of the protection of Kingstown. Governor Seton realised that quick action was needed since the Garifuna at Dorsetshire Hill were in a position to take control of Kingstown and might do so on the following day. Despite having armed some of their slaves there was always concern about the slaves rallying to the side of the Garifuna, especially if they appeared to be in a commanding position.

Governor Seton would have been quite relieved by the timely arrival of forces from Martinique, which was then in the hands of the British. With that reinforcement he felt he needed to act quickly and so those forces, with the local militia and sailors from merchant ships in the bay, met at Sion Hill at midnight on March 14 at the house of a Mr. Hartley. Just past midnight on the morning of March 15, they began their ascent to Dorsetshire Hill under the cover of darkness, with what is described in one source as "the meagre glimmer of a waning moon" (Taylor, p. 121). They succeeded in getting to within 80 yards of the post held by the Garifuna without being recognised. When they were about 20 yards away, the attack was ordered, and the buildings stormed. Shephard states that within 15 minutes "the fate of the hill was determined, the enemy fled in all directions, and through the darkness of the night many of them effected their escape." He stated further that five seamen were killed, and four other soldiers wounded. With the Garifuna and French forces, the numbers of those killed were not given, Shephard simply saying that several were killed. Much emphasis was put on declaring that among those killed was Chatoyer whom he described as "the

Commander-in-Chief of all the forces, for whom "cruelty rather than courage had always been" his principle. In Alexander Anderson's view he was "Generalissimo of the motley band. He was brave, desperate and accustomed to warfare and bloodshed ..." (p. 27).

How did Chatoyer die? Shephard states that he died in "single combat with the brave Major Leith of the militia". Kirby and Martin repeated this and went further stating that Chatoyer had been fully convinced of the legend that he could not be killed by mortal means. Furthermore, "He allowed his vanity to run away with him and he made the fatal mistake of challenging Major Leith to a duel." Leith, they noted, being a trained army officer, would have been "proficient with the sword". From where did this information come? The Garifuna and Kalinago people had left no written accounts, and reports about them were given by the British and French, but even then, none of those sources appears to have given such an account. The issue of Chatoyer, believing that he could not be killed by mortal means, seems very far-fetched. But there is more to be questioned in the account of Chatoyer's death. For a struggle that lasted fifteen minutes, when and how would this duel have been organised? Or perhaps it was spontaneous? Remember, too, that this was in the dark, after one in the morning. The Garifuna and Kalinago warriors traditionally engaged in guerrilla warfare and did not confront their European armies head on. To accept the idea of Chatoyer getting into a duel with Major Leith, given the circumstances, time of day and the brief duration of the encounter, is to stretch the imagination.

But there are other accounts that add to the scepticism of that given by Shephard and Coke before him. It was obvious, too, even from the account given by Shephard, that what occurred was an ambush. The British crept up on them without them being aware until they were 80 yards from their post, and they started firing their shots from 20 yards. The battle, we are told, lasted fifteen minutes.

Extracts from a document "Narrative of the Insurrection in the Island of St. Vincent, March 30, 1795", that might have been taken from the "St. Vincent Gazette", stated in part about the attack on Dorsetshire Hill, "The word march was given at a quarter past 12 o'clock and cheerfully obeyed, the whole party mounting in the preceding order the steep and rugged path in regularity and silence. They ascended within 80 yards of the main post, when they were discovered by a sentry who challenged and fired. The enemy appeared no wise discouraged at the surprise but shouted and opened a smart fire of musquetry (sic) on us. As soon as the party got within twenty yards of the enemy, orders were given to fire a volley and charge. They were obeyed with the greatest vivacity. Captain Skinner and Lieutenant Hill mounted the bank and were immediately followed by the whole detachment of seamen.... The buildings in which the enemy sheltered themselves were stormed and such of them as made resistance were put to the bayonet. Many escaped through the darkness of the night.... The principal share of honour undoubtedly fell to Captain Skinner and Lieutenant Hill of the Zebra, to whom the service owes infinite obligation.... On the side of the enemy, Chatoyer, the Charaib's chief, was killed, with several other Charaibs and inhabitants of French extraction, subjects to his Majesty.... (CO 261/9). No mention is made of any duel or of Major Leith. The persons singled out for praise were Captain Skinner and Lieutenant Hill, with reference also to the roles of Captain Campbell, Lieutenant Groves and Major Whytell. The death of Chatoyer would have been such a prize to the British that his defeat in any duel would certainly have been mentioned and Major Leith singled out.

Governor Seton, in a letter of March 16 ((BA)10. CO 261/6) described the encounter at Dorsetshire Hill, gave similar details. He mentioned that officers, privates and seamen "behaved with the greatest spirit" and he particularly mentions Captains Skynner (sic) and Campbell and Lieutenant McIver, but there was no mention of Major Leith.

There are two later accounts that make specific references to the battle at Dorsetshire Hill. John Anderson, a Scottish lawyer, served as a Special Magistrate in St. Vincent during the period of Apprenticeship and arrived here in January 1836. He left a journal of his stay. This journal, which was deposited at the Aberdeen University Historic Collections, was edited, and published by Roderick McDonald in 2001.

Anderson had taken great pleasure in conversing with aged apprentices, and in listening to the details of their early life. One old lady had witnessed "many of the horrors of the last insurrection of the Caribs". An octogenarian negro recalled being a boy during the 1772 Carib War. Anderson was provided with information about the storming of Dorsetshire Hill on March 14, 1795, by a resident British informant who was then a young man and one of the assailants. His description of the assailants follows those given by the other accounts that have been previously mentioned. His informant recalled that "Not a shot was returned till the gallant little band were within twenty yards of their foe; then they threw in their fire with destructive effect...and in a few minutes were in possession of the post, the enemy flying in every direction, many who escaped bayonet or ball, being dashed to pieces over the precipices." His informant, he said, "was within two rank and file of the cruel Carib Commander-in-Chief Chatoyer, when he fell — Major Leith of the Militia, advanced upon him, crying out, 'You him Chatoyé?' 'Oui B' was the response, accompanied by a thrust of his sword, which was parried, five bayonets being dashed into the sanguinary monster's breast at the same moment" (p. 127-8).

Warner Arundell — The Adventures of a Creole, was a novel by E. L Joseph, best known for his *History of Trinidad*. Arundell was a white creole of British descent who was born in Grenada but brought up in Antigua and Trinidad. Many of the characters in the novel were supposed to have been based on real figures "openly or thinly disguised". A reviewer in the British Metropolitan magazine of February 1838, that was reproduced in the "Trinidad Standard and Port of Spain Gazette" noted that "Joseph's account of incidents always rang true, suggesting that he was informed by actual participants or witnesses, and that he paid 'a nice attention to localities...'" (Joseph, 'Introduction', xxiv).

As a young man Warner was on his way from Grenada to Antigua, the home of his father. His passage organised by his uncle was with the courtesy of Lieutenant Rotherman of His Majesty's Ship Hawk that was going to Antigua but with orders to cruise around the islands. Warner reported that on their way across the channel to St. Vincent from Bequia he recalled a conversation between the Commander and a Mr. Allardice of Canaan (Canouan) "who spoke of many events and anecdotes that each and sometimes both, had been concerned in", including the attack on Dorsetshire Hill (p. 54-55). He described the ascent of Dorsetshire Hill, with them surprising the enemy. He said, "It was no fight — it was a mere regular slaughter; and in a few moments the fort was cleared of the enemy."

The accounts provided by Joseph and Anderson's informant differed from the others only in their references to the Caribs being drunk on the night in question. Anderson's informant indicated that a coloured man of St. Kitts who had escaped from the rebel forces reported to Governor Seton that the Caribs "were surfeiting themselves with the plunder of provisions and liquors, they had seized in their windward march" (p. 127-128). Arundell reported from the conversation by the two participants that "the Caraibes and brigands, after the capture of the post, found a large cargo of spirits stowed away, with which they spliced the main brace; and were as merry and groggy as tars at Portsmouth Point...."

Those two accounts differed on the source of the liquor they were supposed to be enjoying and were the only two sources that made mention of the Caribs enjoying at that critical time the spoils of liquor they had found. The question is, would the Caribs who seemingly intended launching an attack on Kingstown in the morning be drinking and getting themselves groggy at that hour in the morning? Previous accounts of their encounters with the British in the First Carib war and the 1779 joint attack with the French showed a people who went about their business in a serious manner given the fact that they realised that what was at stake was the seizure of their land and their fate.

I have spent some time relating other accounts that differ from that given by Shephard which had been commonly accepted, even by Martin and Kirby. In my 2002 booklet on Chatoyer I stated that it appeared obvious to me that the account of the duel with Major Leith was meant to be a propaganda tool demonstrating British superiority, their Major defeating the exceptional Chatoyer. This is reinforced in my mind by the fact that "under the large chandelier in the Cathedral in Kingstown is a memorial stone placed on the grave of the Major" (Ebenezer Duncan, p. 20). Taylor makes the point to update information supplied by Duncan, that the memorial in the cathedral is now covered by a carpet (p. 159).

The Final Showdown

Two matters that have been neglected in the narrative and discussion about the struggles, particularly of the Garifuna with the British, have to do with the role of the Kalinagos. Were they participants in the 2nd Carib War? Were the indigenous women involved in these battles?

The impression is often given by British sources that the Kalinago people who remained in St. Vincent, though few in numbers, were not participants in what has been referred to as the 2nd Carib War. With French sources now available and giving a different picture this has to be questioned. Frenchman Alexandre Moreau De Jonnes in his *Adventures in the Wars of the Republic and the Consulate* that was published in 1858 when he was 80 years old, described his "first" career as a soldier, serving part of it as a Lieutenant in marine artillery that brought him to St. Vincent to assist in coordinating and training the forces of the indigenous people for a French attack in 1795. He described being met on arrival by Pakiri, the chief of the "Red Caribs" and taken to the middle of the village to a communal house "containing an assembly hall at least 80 feet long" where he found gathered there "the chiefs and warriors of the two tribes, the Red and Black Caribs" (Palacio, p. 37). He had struck up a relationship with Pakiri from whom he gathered that "the defence of his country and the happiness of Eliama were his life" (Palacio, p. 39).

The British colonials argued that they had a more legitimate claim to the lands originally owned and controlled by the Kalinagos because the Garifuna had robbed and taken control of their lands. They then based their supposed legitimacy on the Treaty of Paris of 1763 giving them control of St. Vincent, a treaty in which, of course as indicated before, the indigenous people were not participants and were not involved at any level. It therefore suited the purpose of British commentators on the war to avoid that matter. The scrutiny we are giving to British sources should also be applied to French sources. Having made that point, we have to allow for the fact that the French had a closer relationship with the "Caribs". In the case of Moreau, not only did he help to train combined "Carib" forces, but he participated briefly in the war before being recalled to Guadeloupe, and then to return in 1796 when the British with superior numbers had gained an upper hand. It is my view that the divisions between the Red and Black Caribs (Kalinago and Garifuna) had been exaggerated and projected over the whole span of the existence of the two groups. There appeared also to be confusion distinguishing between the Garifuna, Kalinago and African escaped slaves.

From Moreau De Jonnes we were also informed of the place played by women in the defence of their country. Among the warriors whom he trained were Eliama, daughter of the Yellow Carib chief, Pakiri, and two granddaughters of the Black Carib Chief, Morning Star and Flower of the Forest, whom he said, "never missed a target". Eliama (whose reputation as a warrior, known for her bravery and skill in Martinique and Guadeloupe, having been brought up in a convent in Martinique) had been a frequent visitor to both colonies. He stated that in times of war their "ranks were swelled by their women and girls transformed into bellicose warriors" (quoted by Taylor, p. 184).

Thomas Coke in his *History of the West Indies* (vol. 2, p. 265) had referred to the Carib women as fighters: "Even their women put on a war-like appearance and seem familiarized with the weapons of destruction.... Even in times of peace (they) exhibit an armed neutrality; and both sexes display a state of preparation, either for offensive or defensive war". This role of women has been downplayed or not noted by other British commentators.

The death of Chatoyer impacted seriously in the short and perhaps long run on the Garifuna and Kalinago peoples in their struggle. There was, for a period after the death of Chatoyer, some disunity among the combined forces, with the French combatants from Dorsetshire Hill moving into the area of Layou while the "Caribs" resorted to the lands under their control. The British expected easy victory and tried to capitalise on the demoralised state of French and Garifuna forces. The Garifuna, however, shortly recovered and began their attacks, even at one time setting fire to the estate at Greathead (Arnos Vale). The war continued over another year, with fortunes fluctuating as neither side was able to land a final knock-out. Often it had reached a point of stalemate with the upper hand depending on the timely arrival of forces for either side.

The guerrilla tactics used by the Kalinago and Garifuna people in their struggles with the British, reinforced by their familiarity with the territory, not only annoyed the British but created difficulties for them in combating their forces. Alexander Anderson referred to them as cowards for their manner of fighting. He described their tactics: "They skulked behind trees, in bushes, often in situations no enemy could have supposed they were there. Being the best of marksmen, they seldom missed their aim. Their tawny skin tone rendered them unobservable at a few yards distance. When discovered, their agility (made) any attempt to come up with (them) futile." (p. 68).

In the conversation between Allardice of Canouan and the Commander of the Hawk, as told by Joseph, the Lieutenant was critical of those in charge of the militia and the regulars for marching with their drums beating and colours flying "to fight a savage enemy who crouched like foxes and glided like serpents, from their foes; yet, at unexpected times, daunted like rattlesnakes upon their less vigilant, but better disciplined enemy" (p. 54).

On July 27, 1796, Lieutenant Robert Bassett penned a letter to his father referring to "a horrid butchering war with the Caribs, who neither give nor receive Quarter". He described the Caribs as "an enemy despicable indeed in both courage and numbers but, if considered as to their manner of making war, extremely formidable" (Craton, p. 192). But the situation was beginning to change in favour of the British forces. Perhaps the most critical factor was the arrival of General Abercromby on June 8, 1796, with large forces following their capture of St. Lucia. About 3,960 men were assembled in St. Vincent, the largest ever to be involved in combat in the colony. Two days after, on June 10, an attack against French/"Carib" forces lasted for most of the day. Despite their stubborn resistance, the overwhelming numbers used against them was decisive and led to the French forces under their black Commander, Marinier, sending in a flag of truce and surrendering with promises of also surrendering other posts. The Garifuna moved back into the interior.

Left on their own with a number of other things working against them, some chiefs, by June 15, moved to surrender but argued for the retention of their land, which the British rejected. Some of them asked for time to consult with others and organise their forces to do the same but never responded in the time allowed. The governor, confident under the prevailing circumstances that the Garifuna would not have been able to continue their resistance, declared by proclamation the end of martial law on June 24. While others continued to move in to surrender, some forces still held out and continued to resist. British forces were sent out to capture those who continued their defiance. The month of September was, in fact, devoted to those mopping up operations. This appeared to be a delaying tactic designed to help them to re-establish themselves. Young Chatoyer, son of Chatoyer, was one of those who came forward to surrender but followed this up by leading some of his men into the wooded interior.

Moreau de Jonnes had opted to return to St. Vincent even though he was aware that the end was near because of the superior forces of Abercromby. He said that he was obliged by his honour to do so. He entered at the same point he had done previously and met a desolate situation, having to pass the corpse of dead Indians. When he got near to the area where he had lived he realised that "the enemy had not got so far as this" because things were as he had left them in his hut. He was surprised, however, to have found coming toward him a spaniel which had belonged to the Yellow Carib chief's daughter, Eliama, that was followed by Zami, described as the maid of Eliama. She had hidden with the spaniel in the back of a cave. The other members of the village had died. Eliama who was wounded and had been pursued by "negro enemy trackers" flung herself "into the great fissure of the volcano".

Jonnes was led in the night to one of the last remaining "fortified posts", seemingly under the command of the coloured French officer, Marinier. But with English fighters within range, the situation was a desperate one. "A glance sufficed to show that we have to surrender soon. Food and discipline were equally deficient." Efforts to dislodge British fighters had only partial success and they were left with no alternative but to surrender. Some Caribs had, he stated, opted to seek refuge in Trinidad, using "paddles wrapped in cotton to deaden their sound" (Palacio, p. 42). He reported that one of the Black Carib chiefs, not willing to be taken by the British, "penetrated into the powder magazine and...blew it up, killing himself and others nearby. De Jonnes was wounded and lost consciousness but was assisted by one of the British doctors.

Eventually, by October, most of the forces had surrendered.

The British strategies in the end gave them a decided advantage. The armed slaves, known as the Rangers, proved to be quite effective in burning canoes and destroying provision grounds. They were able to get into areas that their regular soldiers could not. Moreau de Jonnes, in explaining what he considered the reasons for the defeat of the "Caribs" gave quite a lot of credit to the use of negroes from Martinique who were led by two Creoles that were accustomed to hunting slaves in the woods. He said that "These negroes crept at full length through passages believed to be inaccessible, and, getting in rear of the last military position, they reached the redoubt, which served as a refuge for the women and children and a storehouse for munitions and food. They sacked everything, pitilessly killing the harmless occupants, pillaging, and burning the foodstuffs...."

The destruction of their provision grounds made them dependent on supplies of food from Martinique, and once the British were able to block their route they were left in a desperate situation. An urgent request was made by one of the generals on July 7 for 500 negroes "with bills and cutlasses to destroy the provisions in the Charaib Country" (Taylor, p. 137). The destruction of provision grounds thus appeared to have been a critical factor in the decision of the Garifuna forces to surrender since with British control of some of their communication points, like Owia, communication with the French was extremely difficult if not, under the circumstances, virtually impossible.

On the effectiveness of the Rangers Anderson wrote, "The corps of blacks that were formed were in a great measure the preservation of the island. They were always on the most severe and dangerous service and always behaved well, nor (I believe), an instance of an individual of them ever deserting to the enemy. They were headed, it is true, by brave and hardy officers from the militia" (p. 74).

To Balliceaux and Ruattan

Following the lifting of Martial Law on June 24, a meeting of the Colonial Assembly was held, but this had been preceded by a meeting between inhabitants where a decision was taken to send the Carib prisoners to Balliceaux as a temporary holding place, the proprietor Campbell giving consent. Orders for the removal to Balliceaux were given on July 15 by General Abecromby, and the process began shortly after and was not completed until October when the last resistance ended.

It was estimated that between July 1796 and February 1797, some 4,338 Carib prisoners were taken to Balliceaux; 1,004 men, 1779 women and 1,555 children. The British ship "Experiment" arrived on February 25, 1797, to take the "prisoners" to Ruattan, but left on March 9 after spending three days in Bequia. Only 2,248 eventually left. The original list might have included "Yellow Caribs", some of whom, it was said, were sent back to the mainland of St. Vincent. Those numbers were small, indicating that a significant number had died on Mustique, mostly it appears, from disease. The "Caribs" who remained in St. Vincent believed that the deaths were deliberate. "Captain George" a "Black Carib" told Ornithologist Frederick Ober during a visit to Sandy Bay sometime between 1876 and 1878 that the British "caused lime to be mixed in their bread." Ober did not accept this and felt that it probably arose from "the water being impregnated with lime, caused much sickness and death" (*Camps in the Caribbees*, p. 216-7).

Balliceaux, a small island of the Grenadines, was without a source of water and lacked springs and streams. Water had to be transported from Kingstown. As one looks at Balliceaux today, it is difficult to imagine how over 4,000 "Caribs" would have been able to survive for the few months they were kept there. Anderson tried to convey the impression that they were equipped with all the conveniences possible. "Buildings and every possible accommodation were provided for them, canoes and fishing tackle for those that chose to catch fish for their families…" He stated too that "vessels were in constant employ by the island in carrying them provisions and water" and a surgeon from the garrison had been in place to take care of the sick (p 227, Hulme et al). He was trying to refute "any imputation of cruelty or inhuman treatment…."

Although some British commentators attributed the deaths to many of the Caribs being sent to Balliceaux in an emaciated condition arising from the war, where they had held out for so long before surrendering, it appears obvious that the limited space and inhospitable conditions, including unavailability of water and adequate food, would have contributed to the spread of disease. It must be pointed out, too, that a number of British soldiers died, apparently over 13.

On March 9, the Garifuna population left their homeland after a long struggle to protect it. Although the overwhelming majority would have been Garinagu, some Kalinagos were likely to have been among the group sent into exile. This was not the end of resistance for there were "Caribs" who had not surrendered, but held out in the interior. They continued to present problems to the British inhabitants. At a meeting of the Legislative Council on September 4, 1798, President Drewry Ottley informed the body that they were then in a position to undertake the expedition against the "Caribs" that had been delayed because of the violent rains. What was needed was some 40 negro pioneers to join their troops, but with the proviso that the deaths or in case of those disabled, the proprietor would have been reimbursed (BA.CO 260/16, 18 July 1798).

Reports of attacks on persons and plantations had been drawn to their attention. A Mr. Clapham who was planting on lands at Grand Sable was murdered by "Caribs" while at Rabacca. President Ottley had later drawn attention to the murder of a private of the West India Regiment by a small party of "Caribs" (Ottley, September 6, 1799, in CO 260/16, Whitehall, November 14, 1799).

In 1802 Grand Sable was described as a haven for runaways. "...in its present state however it is a harbour for all runaways and the black Charaibs whose haunts are almost inaccessible; will render it difficult to preserve the Colony in case of insurrection and make it an easy prey by an enemy." (CO 261/18. "Precis of Correspondence", St. Vincent 19 October 1802 [private]. A negro field slave who had run away from the Hope estate encountered a community of negro runaway slaves and "Caribs". About half of them she suggested were "Caribs". She was unable to indicate to the proprietors after she escaped the location of the camp, since she had been blindfolded and taken there. She escaped by following the course of the river and came out below Gordon. The Legislative Council had resolved to have a two-man committee organise the raising of slaves from the leeward estates to assist in search of the camp. It resolved "that the Negroes shall be fed and the same hire and rewards given as by the Resolution of this House as of 23 March, 1803. To which they request the concurrence of your Board and that you will appoint a member thereof to join the above-named gentlemen (of the Committee) to carry the same into effect." (January 31, 1805, W. Struth, Speaker; CO 260/19, 1805. Meeting of Council, Thursday 31, January 1805).

The search for "Caribs" continued. An Act passed in June 1804 declared that the Caribs had forfeited all claims to lands they had been entitled to by the 1773 Treaty. Some Carib children and a mother were captured, and others surrendered. An Act of 1805 issued a pardon and gave lands to them at Morne Ronde. Other Caribs held out, including some that Kirby and Martin stated had taken up lands in Greiggs. This was really the end of the resistance. No one was sure about the number of Caribs who had remained after the major expulsion of 1797. Even the censuses had been quite inadequate in determining the numbers. There is still a story that needs to be told about those who remained and continued to be a part of the Vincentian society. Descendants of those sent into exile and those who remained hold common ground today in having Chatoyer as their national hero and in seeking to have Balliceaux turned into a museum in honour of their fore-parents who had fought heroically to maintain the independence of a country they considered their own. Chatoyer was portrayed by his enemies as cruel and bloodthirsty, really as a villain. The now independent state of St. Vincent and the Grenadines has seen it fit to declare Chatoyer its first national hero, something that was applauded by descendants in the Central American diaspora.

Tombstone in Anglican Church in Hulme, Peter and Neil Whitehead, Ed., Wild Majesty Encounters with Caribs from Columbus to Present Day— An Anthology. *Oxford: Clarendon Press, 1992.*

Chapter 6
Epilogue:
From Villain to National Hero

Until the lions have their historians, tales of hunting will always glorify the hunter.

- African Proverb

When the decision was made to provide the country with its first Vincentian national hero and to establish a National Heroes Day, it was informed by a long period of advocacy that provided a general consensus that Chatoyer, paramount chief of the Garifuna and Kalinago people should be the country's first national hero. It was widely agreed that the date for National Heroes Day, which was to be a public holiday, would have been the date on which Chatoyer was killed. The long period of advocacy had virtually eliminated any other contenders. Although there was little detailed knowledge about the man, Chatoyer (Chatawae), what he stood for and represented had seeped into the consciousness of a large number of Vincentians.

The collapse of the West Indian Federation in 1961 and the decision of Jamaica and Trinidad and Tobago to become independent as individual countries in 1962, sparked a wide debate about independence for the smaller countries that were still colonies of Britain. Part of the conversation centred around the practicality of independence for small colonies. A UN resolution of 1960, which declared that size should not be an impediment to independence, influenced the debate that followed.

St. Vincent had become a colony of Britain in 1763 and recovered its independence in 1979 after 216 years of colonial control. The conversation about the establishment of National Heroes Day with Chatoyer as the first national hero had started before 1979, but independence in that year introduced a different set of dynamics and gave a solid base to those ideas. An independent country with the basic structures of colonialism still intact needed to reconstruct its society and develop its own identity and personality. Independence on October 27, 1979, was a significant event that set in motion a process, still continuing, that involved creating a society that catered to the hopes and aspirations of all its people; a society that gave due recognition to its indigenous peoples and that would rehabilitate the Carib Chief Chatoyer and his people and remove them from the historical dust bin.

Changes in the educational system and in particular, new historical perspectives, put all of these into a different context. To many of the older people the initial reaction was either nonchalance or direct rejection. They grew up under a system where information from books was supposed to be absolute and sacrosanct. To question anything and present new perspectives was to question their education and leave them exposed. So the fact that the history books informed them that Christopher Columbus discovered St. Vincent on January 22, 1498, was not to be questioned. Initially the idea of Chatoyer as a national hero made them very wary, for in the colonial texts he was painted as savage and brutal. But even more, deep within their psyche they still recognised persons such as Christopher Columbus and Drake and Hawkins as heroes.

The period 1763 to 1979 was one of direct colonial control, at least up to 1969 when the country became a State in Association with Britain. But what did colonial control involve? A very critical area of control as identified by the Kenyan writer, Ngugi Wá Thiongo, was the "mental universe". He described it as "control through culture, of how people define themselves and their relationship to the world" (p. 16 *Decolonising the Mind*). Culture was for him a "bomb" that encompassed "moral, ethical and aesthetic values, the set of spiritual eyeglasses through which they come to view themselves and their place in the universe" (p. 14-15). This was the "mental slavery" that Bob Marley warned about in his "Redemption Song".

The independence of former colonies achieved through peaceful means and often dictated by the "Mother Country" is often described as "flag independence", that is largely about the changing of flags and national anthems and the heads of government being termed "Governor General" rather than "Governor". But independence is much more. It is about a process that involves "emancipating ourselves from mental slavery", again quoting Bob Marley. This involves the people seeing themselves free from colonialism with the challenge of defining their own identity and creating a path to their own development as an independent entity.

Central to all this was colonial education, what Wá Thiongo considered the "psychological violence of the classroom" that defined our indigenous and colonial peoples as objects rather than subjects of their history. Rex Nettleford took this further and argued that in a post-colonial society our history had to be "rewritten and reconstructed through one's own eyes" (Nettleford, p. 101, *Caribbean*

Quarterly). This meant overturning much of what was learnt and beginning to see things from the perspective of post-colonial peoples. It also demanded, among other things, to look again at people who were presented to us as heroes and replace them by heroes as identified by ourselves.

In St. Vincent, one of the first significant things that came out of this rethinking and re-examination of our colonial education, was the rejection of what had become accepted truth, that Christopher Columbus had "discovered" St. Vincent. Quite apart from the fact that Columbus was in Spain on January 22, 1498, when he was supposed to have "discovered" the country, there was also the issue of the concept of "discovery", which was to some extent a part of European arrogance and mythology, which people of the country had bought into for a long time.

As Vincentians discussed and debated the idea of Independence, issues about black consciousness and black identity that came with the Black Power Movement became part of the conversation. As the Americas prepared to celebrate in 1992 the quincentenary of the arrival of Columbus in what was dubbed the "New World", the debate about the struggles of the indigenous peoples was awakened and they attempted to define their own history and correct the Eurocentric distortions. Chatoyer, as a "Black Carib" — as he had been classified — fitted into this blending of black power and identity and indigenous reawakening and "rediscovery". The Caribbean Organisation of Indigenous Peoples (COIP), of which St. Vincent was a member, came out of this reawakening. It provided opportunities for the Garifuna of St. Vincent to strengthen their links with those of Belize, who were descendants of the indigenous people exiled in 1797.

The political, cultural and historical forces merged to occasion a re-examination of the colonial textbooks that portrayed the people as objects rather than subjects of their history. Charles Shephard had suggested that the history of these colonies was of little importance: "The early history of the lesser colonies in the West Indies is so obscure, and of such little importance in the present age, that it is hardly worthy of any research; there are few records to be found in any writings of those who first visited them, *which are not either enveloped in fiction, or distorted by ignorance or prejudice*" (p. 19, my emphasis). Ironically this applied to his own writings.

With the decision to make March 14 National Heroes Day, the existing "Discovery and National Heroes Day", celebrated on January 22, had to be abolished. In 1973 an effort was made by the government led by James Mitchell to abolish the holiday, which was then celebrated as "Discovery Day". There was a strong political fallout from this as established groups in the country strenuously objected. Prime Minister Mitchell — as he later became — rechristened the day "Discovery and National Heroes Day". That was an absurdity for an independent country made up of descendants of the people who populated the country at the time of the arrival of the Europeans and of the people of African descent who were brought here following the genocidal efforts of the Europeans.

The first recognition of Chatoyer as an important historical figure occurred in 1823. It came in the form of a play, "The Drama of King Shotaway", founded on Facts taken from the "Insurrection of the Caravs on the Island of St. Vincent", which was believed to have been written by a Mr Brown. Unfortunately, only the playbill remains, since no known copy of the play has been found. The play was performed at the African Grove Theatre in New York and is said to be the first about a black person and written by a black person who became recognized as the father of Black Theatre in the United States of America. The title of the play leads one to conclude that the author had experienced it and therefore might have been a Garinagu. Christopher Taylor has raised some questions about Brown's experience of the events about which he had written. He said that in 1822 the play was actually first presented by Brown as "Shotaway; or the Drama of the Caribs of St. Domingo". While this could lead us to raise questions about Brown's origin and experience of the insurrection, he might have been provided with first-hand information that provided the text of his play. In any event the author considered 'Shotaway' (Chatoyer) important enough to be the subject of his play.

Today one of the things that unites the Garifuna of St. Vincent and the Grenadines and those of Central America, is the recognition of Chatoyer as National Hero. Over the years there has been a reconnection of the Vincentian Garifuna and those of Central America. Because of the fact that the English language is commonly spoken in Belize and St. Vincent, Belize has been at the forefront of that reconnection. In 1951 Ronald Harvey Garvey, as governor of British Honduras, (later Belize) addressed the Settlement Day ceremony there. Garvey had been before this, from 1944-49, administrator of St. Vincent. He informed the gathering that on his arrival in St. Vincent he realised that not all of the "Black Caribs" (Garifuna) had been sent into exile in Central America but that in St. Vincent there remained "Black and Yellow Caribs". He told the gathering "Your kinsmen who still live in that Colony also possess many of your excellent characteristics of fortitude and energy. Like you, yourselves, they are interested in the natural pursuits of agriculture and fishing, and they contribute as you do to learning by turning out many excellent school teachers" (Guillick, p. 193). Later, in 1966, the Mayor of Stann Creek extended an invitation to the Chief Minister of St. Vincent, the Honourable Ebenezer Joshua, to send a Carib delegation to participate in their "Settlement Day" of that year, to be held on November 19. Three Caribs from Sandy Bay were sent, Mr Bracken, Mrs Francoise and Mr Rene Child.

From the 1960s, Chatoyer as someone worthy of National Heroes Status, had begun to seep into the consciousness of Vincentians. An individual masquerader, Louis Boucher had, in 1963 and 1973, depicted Chatoyer as national hero in his presentations for 'Individual Mas' during the Carnival celebrations. Political activist and later Minister of Government, Eddie Griffith had, in 1972, named his first daughter, Yulu (Youlou), the name it was then believed was used for St. Vincent by the indigenous people. One of the minor political parties that arose out of a period of political activism in the 1960s and 70s was named "Yulimo" (Youlou United Liberation Movement). Some calypsonians had highlighted Chatoyer in their calypsos for the carnival celebrations.

The National Youth Council and other voluntary and non-governmental organisations and individuals had started advocating for Chatoyer to be named national hero. This bore some fruit on March 14, 1985, when an Obelisk was unveiled by Minister of Culture, John Horne, at a ceremony at Dorsetshire Hill near to the site where Chatoyer was alleged to have been killed. The plaque for the Obelisk was donated by the government of Venezuela, through the instrumentality of the former Charge d'Affaires, Jorge Gonzalez and Ambassador Moanack. The event was chaired by Junior Bacchus, a member of the National Youth Council. In attendance were the Charge d' Affaires of the Venezuelan Embassy, Victor Croquer and representatives of government, the National Youth Council, the National Trust and other organisations and individuals. The need for a statue to be placed at some conspicuous place in Kingstown was suggested by the President of the National Trust, Arthur Connell, and was to be undertaken by the government of Venezuela. At the ceremony Chatoyer was, by many, unofficially declared National Hero.

In this new awakening, Chatoyer, who had been described in the most derogatory terms by colonial writers, was now being seen as an heroic figure worthy of the status of a national hero. In the early struggles of the indigenous people as they confronted the forces unleashed by Columbus, the indigenous people of St. Vincent stood out as the last defenders against European encroachment. Long after other colonies had become colonies of Europe and were transformed into sugar colonies, St. Vincent continued to battle those who were trying to invade its shores. Although the country became a colony of Britain in 1763, the British only had partial control, the Garifuna and Kalinagos remaining resolute about their ownership.

In 1768 Chatoyer made his first appearance in the historical literature as one of the leaders of the resistance when, at Grand Sable, he asked who was that king of "Great Britain" that was laying claim to their lands. He knew no such king! The envoy sent by the British was told that he should "retire whilst in safety" for Chatoyer had spoken on behalf of all of them. Although in a leadership position, it was not clear if he was Chief of Grand Sable or of one of the other areas under "Carib" control. In the 1773 treaty that came at the end of the First "Carib War", he was just listed as one of the chiefs; but the works of Sir William Young and Charles Shephard indicated that he was clearly the chief spokesman and remained so until his death in 1795. He was later shown as chief strategist and identified at some point as paramount chief. In 1768 the Garifuna were the numerically dominant of the indigenous peoples and assumed control of the resistance. As paramount chief he also assumed control of the Kalinago forces.

What stood out for Vincentians as they advocated for his elevation as first national hero was his unyielding spirit. As they reflected and empathized with the people of that time, the reality was that a people described as barely human, in fact, as savages, were able with "primitive" weapons to stand against the European powerhouse of that time. As they highlighted the role and leadership of Chatoyer, the reality was that the struggle was started by the Kalinagos long before Chatoyer and the Garifuna appeared on the scene. It has to be recognised, too, that although shaken by the death of their leader, the indigenous people, with French help, were able to continue the struggle for about a year after before succumbing to the superior numbers and weaponry of the British forces.

After a long period of advocacy that called not only for Chatoyer to be the first national hero but for a National Heroes Day holiday, an indication that formal recognition was coming, was the declaration of March 14, 2001, as a holiday. The general elections shortly after, which saw the New Democratic Party being replaced by the Unity Labour Party, eventually led to March 14, 2002, being declared as National Heroes Day and Chatoyer as the First National Hero of St. Vincent and the Grenadines. The Order of National Heroes Act 2002 that listed the criteria for conferring the honour, was assented to by Governor General Sir Charles Antrobus on February 25, 2002, but a significant section of the Vincentian population had already determined who it was going to be, so it might be that the life and exploits of Chatoyer, as reconstructed, informed the act.

A national hero was thought to be one who was a national symbol and whose service and struggles can inspire the people of the nation even after 200 years; an individual who became a "beacon of hope". His was an unyielding spirit that with inferior weaponry led his people for over 27 years in an effort to recover their independence. He could therefore be described as the father of Independence. Although the Kalinago people had long struggled against European encroachment, when Chatoyer appeared on the scene the English had already been given control of the island by the Treaty of Paris of 1763. The circumstances are different today but the stubborn resistance for such a long period despite overwhelming odds makes its own statement. Chatoyer understood the geopolitics of the time and sought French assistance in the struggles of his people.

The manner in which his European enemies described him as brutal, brave, ruthless, desperate, and accustomed to warfare strengthened the positive image the people had of him, for he was fighting for his people. As a people fighting to reconstruct their history and to combat the legacies of colonialism, the bitter terms in which Chatoyer was portrayed by his enemies could not but endear him to them and allow for his rehabilitation from the pens of his enemies. Sir William Young recognised him as the one with whom he had to contend. Sir William Young, junior, referred to the "flattering attentions and hospitality" that Chatoyer, his family or tribe, received from his father. He even brought to St. Vincent the Italian artist Agostino Brunias who painted a picture of Chatoyer and his five wives that is the physical image we have of him today. When the younger Sir William visited St. Vincent after his father's death he appeared to have cultivated Chatoyer's friendship and even described a visit to his home with Duvallee and their sons.

The French had tremendous confidence in Chatoyer and allowed their men to serve under his leadership in the 2nd Carib War. He played a leading role in the 1779 capture of St. Vincent by the French and participated in the treaty arrangements that followed. The French were obviously impressed with him as a military strategist and the respect that his people had for him. In their struggles against the British in the two "English Carib" wars, the Garifuna and Kalinago forces had for long confounded the British with their guerrilla tactics. These tactics were not new but assumed major importance in a struggle with the British who were then fighting them on their own land. Not prepared to confront the superior military weaponry of the British they used what was most appropriate for them, given their familiarity with the landscape. Chatoyer, it appeared, was able to marshal his forces in a way that frustrated the British. From the pens of his enemies, we are able to conclude that he was a major strategist, something I have suggested was recognised by the French. His death had, for a short period after, left their forces in a state of apprehension. So accustomed to his leadership were the French that for a brief time after his death they felt all was lost. But as homage is paid to Chatoyer, it also has to be recognised that he personified his people, whose struggles began before him; he brought his strategic and organisational talent to the struggle. As Fabel states, "Chatoyé seems to have been their chief organizer, spokesman, and perhaps, military strategist. He insisted on consultation and consensus..." (Fabel p. 207).

The life of Chatoyer has much to teach us and this was recognised by the then Leader of the Opposition, the Honourable Arnhim Eustace who, in 2003 at the wreath laying ceremony at Dorsetshire Hill, stated that the Vincentian people needed the spirit of Chatoyer to grapple with most of the problems they faced as a nation. The

Prime Minister, Dr the Honourable Ralph Gonsalves suggested that the best way to honour Chatoyer was to fully understand what he stood for.

Perhaps what best exemplifies the strength and significance of Chatoyer was the tribute the British were prepared to give to Major Leith for allegedly defeating him in a hand to hand combat. This version of his death is now thoroughly discounted. Kenneth John's perspective on this is worth recalling, "in order to glorify and add lustre to their feat British historians had Chatoyer falling in hand-to-hand combat with their own Major Alexander Leith. If that story had been true, and the entire scene not conjured up...one could have rest assured that Chatoyer's body would have been paraded mockingly as a trophy of war and his place of internment marked as a stain to native pretensions. Instead, to this day nobody knows where the remains of Chatoyer lie.... It was important to the British that we should be deprived of the psychological uplift that comes with having native heroes to worship. They therefore tried to sweep the cupboard bare..." (March 15, 2002, *The Vincentian*).

The Right Excellent Paramount Chief, Chatoyer

(Searchlight photo)

When one takes into account the fact that the other countries that were populated by the indigenous people had long come under the control of the British and French, the fact that in St. Vincent, they were able to hold out for over 30 years after the British had acquired a hold on the country, must owe something to their astute leadership, especially given the fact that the British were hell bent on acquiring lands for the production of sugar. Chatoyer left for us an indomitable spirit of resistance, extreme confidence and self-assurance and an understanding of the geopolitics of his time. He understood his environment and led his forces using guerrilla tactics that frustrated the English steeped in their conventional military warfare approaches.

At a ceremony at Victoria Park at midnight on March 13, 2002, "National Heroes" Day was ushered in and The Right Excellent Paramount Chief Joseph Chatoyer was declared the First National Hero of St. Vincent and the Grenadines. The Order of National Heroes

Act, 2002, that identified the criteria by which a national hero is proclaimed stated as follows:

(10) "In determining the qualification...the Committee (the National Heroes Advisory Committee) shall have regard to whether that person;

a) Has given outstanding service to Saint Vincent and the Grenadines and his contribution has altered positively the course of the history of Saint Vincent and the Grenadines.

b) Has given service to Saint Vincent and the Grenadines which has been exemplified by visionary and pioneering leadership, extraordinary achievement and the attainment of the highest excellence which has redounded to the honour of Saint Vincent and the Grenadines; or

c) Has, through his heroic exploits and sacrifice contributed to the improvement of the economic, social or political conditions of Saint Vincent and the Grenadines and Vincentians generally."

There was, of course, little doubt that he fitted those categories.

The *Searchlight* newspaper, of March 15, 2002, captured the moment: "In the first seconds of March 14 at Victoria Park, Kingstown, St. Vincent, Prime Minister, Dr Ralph Gonsalves, unveiled a larger than life size depiction of the newly installed hero. A tinge of pride and accomplishment overflowed the arena and filled those present with relief. Dr Gonsalves citing Chatoyer as 'fighter for self-determination, and independence, who has given service to St. Vincent and the Grenadines, exemplified by visionary and pioneering leadership, extra-ordinary achievement and the attainment of the highest excellence which has redounded to the honour of St. Vincent and the Grenadines' made the declaration."

In his opening remarks, Prime Minister Gonsalves stated, "We are a people forged from the bowels of slavery, indentureship and colonialism. We are a people who after centuries of oppression have risen to chart our own destiny and regain our independence. We are gathered here to honour one son of the soil who through his unselfish deeds and sacrifice has contributed immensely to the development of our country and the advancement of our Caribbean Civilisation."

Then followed the reading of the citation by the Prime Minister. Something obviously went wrong with the research that informed the citation. Chatoyer is described as the Paramount Chief of the Kalinago People while it is commonly agreed that Chatoyer was a member of the Garifuna community or as they were called then, the 'Black Caribs'. The citation briefly summarizes the struggles of the "Carib" people and completely leaves out the Garifuna. It is known that when the British were given rights to St. Vincent in 1763, the Kalinago people ("Yellow Caribs") were few in number. The fight for the recovery of the independence of St. Vincent was thus under the control of the Garifuna people, with participation undoubtedly by the Kalinagos who remained. It might perhaps be advisable to rewrite the citation even if for historical accuracy and to avoid any confusion that might arise.

Final Note

Despite attempts to select other national heroes, nothing, as of the time of the writing of this monograph, has been finalised. The reasons are not clear. There is a view by some persons, including this author, that Chatoyer has not yet been given his due. While on March 14 every year the wreath laying ceremonies continue and tributes are paid to Chatoyer, there is still a great deal left to do in creating a greater understanding of Chatoyer as leader of the struggles against the British. At the wreath laying ceremony on March 14, 2007, the Minister of Culture, Ms. Rene Baptiste, who described Chatoyer as "a legend in history who equals and surpasses people such as Churchill, Wilberforce, Newton and Einstein," informed the gathering that a grant from the U.S. Embassy was to be used to research the life of Chatoyer, with plans being made "to produce a documentary on the Chief which she would attempt to have shown on the History and National Geographic Channels" (Sheron Garraway, *Searchlight*, March 16, 2007).

There are a number of people, perhaps more than was previously realised, who resent the idea of the country's national hero being depicted dressed in loin cloth. To have this point of view is to attempt to take Chatoyer out of the times in which he lived and to recreate him in the life of a 20th or 21st century being. Chatoyer was an 18th century leader whose mission was to fight colonial rule. Up to the time he died, his people still had control over their own lives, accommodating where necessary the fact that a foreign power had taken hold of part of their country. There is also scepticism about the reality of a person called Chatoyer, since as far as is known the name Chatoyer does not exist in this country. This question has quite often been posed to me and the simple answer is that the majority of Garifuna and Kalinago people were removed from this country. It is known historically that Chatoyer had children and one of his sons was among those who were sent into exile. The fact that some of these matters come up is testimony to continuing lack of awareness about the history of our early peoples. Having said that, it must be pointed out that the Garifuna Heritage Foundation has been holding annual conferences on which issues related to the Garifuna and Kalinago people are discussed. It might be that enough has not been presented on Chatoyer himself, but in any event, it has to be noted that the attendance of local people at these conferences leaves much to be desired.

Other important things have been happening. The links and connections with the Garinagu of Central America, particularly Belize have been strengthened and cultural shows involving Garifuna dancers have been held. Balliceaux, that island in the Grenadines where the Garifuna and Kalinago people were kept before being sent into exile, has become a sacred ground for their descendants and a call has been made to turn it into a National Museum.

This year, on October 27, 2019, St. Vincent and the Grenadines will be commemorating 40 years as an independent nation, or better stated, 40 years since it recovered its independence. In reflecting on this we need to remember that our national hero, Chatoyer, led the early struggle for the recovery of our country's independence. This book is therefore dedicated to the 40th anniversary of Independence and shows Chatoyer's role in that early struggle.

Bibliography

Books

Beckles, Hilary McD and Verene Shepherd. *Liberties Lost – Caribbean Indigenous Societies and Slave Systems*. Cambridge: Cambridge University Press, 2004

Coke, Thomas. *A History of the West Indies containing the Natural, Civil and Ecclesiastical History of Each Island : with an Account of the Missions Instituted in those islands, from the commencement of their civilisation...* Vol. 1 (3 volumes): London, 1808-1811.

Craton, Michael. *Testing the Chains: Resistance to Slavery in the British West Indies*. New York:

Cornell University Press, 1982.

Davidson, George. "The Case of the Caribbs in St. Vincent". 1787. Ed. Coke. London

De Silva, Mark. *The French Church & The Caribs: A Brief History of the early Roman Catholic Church in St. Vincent and the Grenadines* 1652-1797. Kingstown, St. Vincent and the Grenadines, 2010.

Duncan, Ebenezer. *A Brief History of St. Vincent with Studies in Citizenship*. Kingstown, St. Vincent (n.p) 1941.

Eaden, John. ed. *The Memoirs of Pere Labat* 1693- 1705. London: Frank Cass and Co. Ltd, 1970.

Ellis, Godsman. *The Garinagu of Belize*. Belize: The Haman Belize, 1997.

Edwards, Bryan *The History, Civil and Commercial of the British Colonies in the West Indies*, 4th Edition, vol. 1. London: John Stockdale, 1807.

Fabel, Robin F. A . *Colonial Challenges: Britons, Native Americans and Caribs, 1759-1775*. Gainesville: University Press of Florida, 2000.

Fraser, Adrian *Chatoyer (Chatawae) National Hero of St. Vincent and the Grenadines:* Kingstown: Galaxy Printery, 2010.

Gonzalez, Nancie *Sojourners of the Caribbean – Ethnogenesis and Ethnohistory of the Garifuna.* Chicago: University of Illinois Press, 1988.

Goveia, Elsa. *A Study on the Historiography of the British West Indies to the end of the Nineteenth Century.* Mexico: Instituto Panamericano de Geografia E Historia, 1956.

Gullick, C. J. M. *Myths of a Minority – Changing Traditions of the Vincentian Caribs.* Assen: Van Gorcum, 1985.

Honychurch, Lennox. *Negre Mawon – The Fighting Maroons of Dominica.* Dominica: Paramount Printers Ltd., 2014.

The Dominica Story – A History of the Island. (3rd.ed.) London: Macmillan Education Ltd, 1995.

Howard, Richard A and Elizabeth S (1981) ed. Alexander Anderson, *Geography and History of St. Vincent, West Indies.* London: Harvard College and Linnean Society, 1981.

Hulme, Peter, and Neil Whitehead. Ed. *Wild Majesty – Encounters with Caribs from Columbus to Present Day –* An Anthology. Oxford: Clarendon Press, 1992.

Joseph, E.L. *Warner Arundell – The Adventures of a Creole.* edited by Lise Winer. Jamaica: University of the West Indies Press, 2001.

Kirby, I. E. and C. I. Martin. *The Rise and Fall of the Black Caribs:* Kingstown, St. Vincent, 1972.

Le Breton, Fr. Adrien (1662-1736) *The Caribs of St. Vincent: Historic Account of Saint Vincent and the Indian Youroumayn, the Island of the Caribs*. edited by Mark de Silva, with introduction by Fr. Robert Divonne. Kingstown, (np), 2018.

Marshall, Barnard. *Slavery, Law and Society in the British Windward Islands 1763-1823*. Kingston, Jamaica: Arawak Publications, 2007.

Mc Donald, Roderick. Ed. *Between Slavery and Freedom – Special Magistrate John Anderson's Journal of Saint Vincent during the Apprenticeship*. Jamaica: University of the West Indies Press, 2001.

Moreau De Jonnes, Alexandre. *Adventures in the Wars of the Republic and the Consulate 1858*. Ardy, A.J: London: John Murray, 1920.

Ngugi, Wa Thiong'O. *Decolonising the Mind – The Politics of Language in African Literature*: London: James Currey, 1981.

Ober, Fred. "Camps in the Caribbees". Boston: Lee and Shephard, 1880.

Palacio, Joseph. *The Garifuna: A Nation across Borders*. Essays in Social Anthropology. Belize: Cubola Productions, 2005.

Rampersad, Sabrian and James Robertson ed. "Caribbean Archaeology and Material Culture" in *Caribbean Quarterly* vol. 55, No 2. June 2009. Kingston, Jamaica.

Sauer, Carl Ortwin. *The Early Spanish Main*. California: University of California Press, 1966.

Shephard, Charles. *An Historical Account of the Island of Saint Vincent*. London: Frank Cass and Company Ltd, 1997.

Taylor, Christopher (2012) *The Black Carib Wars: Freedom, Survival and the Making of the Garifuna*. Jackson: University of Mississippi, 2012.

Van der Plas, D. Gualbert (1654) *The History of the Massacre of Two Jesuit Missionaries in the Island of St. Vincent, 24 January 1654*. (nd). Kingstown, St. Vincent: The Government Printery.

Waters, Ivor. *The Unfortunate Valentine Morris*. Chepstow Society, Chepstow, 1964

Young, Sir William (1971) *An Account of the Black Charaibs in the Island of St. Vincent's – with The Charaib Treaty of 1773 and other Original Documents*, compiled from the Papers of Sir William Young. London: Frank Cass and Company Ltd, 1971.

Articles and chapters from Books

Beckles, Hilary McD. "Kalinago (Carib) Resistance to European Colonisation of the Caribbean". *Caribbean Quarterly*, Vol. 38, Nos. 2&3, 1992. Mona, Jamaica: University of the West Indies, 1994.

Fraser, Adrian. "Joseph Chatoyer". *Caribbean Trailblazers St. Vincent and the Grenadines*, edited by Baldwin King and Cheryl Phills King. Eugene, Oregon: Kingstown, St. Vincent and the Grenadines Publishers, 2010.

"Revisiting the Carib Story". *Caribbean Quarterly – a Journal of Caribbean Culture*, vol. 60, no. 2, p. 53-64: University of the West Indies, 2014.

Gonzalez, Nancie "The Garifuna of Central America". Samuel Wilson ed. *"The People of the Caribbean"*, University Press of Florida: Gainesville, 1997.

John, Kenneth. "Searching for National Heroes". *The Vincentian*. Kingstown, March 21, 2003.

Kirby, Earle. "Pre-Columbian Indians in St. Vincent, West Indies". St. Vincent Archaeological and Historical Society: Kingstown, 1971.

Lawrence, Harold. "Mandinga Voyages across the Atlantic". Ivan Van Sertima ed. *African Presence in Early America: Journal of African Civilizations*, Rutgers University, 1987.

Marshall, Barnard "The Black Caribs – Native Resistance to British Penetration into the Windward Side of St. Vincent, 1763-

1773". *Caribbean Quarterly*, University of the West Indies: Mona, Jamaica. 1973

Nettleford, Rex. "Surviving Columbus – Caribbean Achievements in the Encounter of Worlds 1492-1992", "Caribbean Quincentennial". *Caribbean Quarterly*, Vol. 38, Nos. 2& 3, 1992.

Sparling, Wilcox, "The Historical Geography of St. Vincent" (MA diss., Carleton University, 1970).

"William Young's Tour of the Islands (1791)", pgs. 210-215.

Hulme, Peter, and Neil Whitehead ed. *Wild Majesty – Encounters with Caribs from Columbus to the Present Day* – An Anthology. New York: Oxford University Press, 1992.

OFFICIAL PUBLICATIONS

British Archives

BA. CO 260/13 XC/A 63011 – A Proclamation by James Seton, Capt. General and Governor in Chief of St. Vincent and the Grenadines, March 20, 1795.

CO 261/5 67 (May 24, 1789. "Letter from Hartley for payment for the rental of houses belonging to him on Dorsetshire Hill that had been occupied by the King's troops" to Governor Seton.

CO 261/6- Letter from Governor Seton re Ambush of Caribs on Dorsetshire Hill and Death of Chatoyer, March 16 (10)

CO 261/9 Narrative of the Insurrection of the Island of St. Vincent, March 30, 1795.

The case of the Caribs in St. Vincent – Letter, Dublin April 18, 1788. The Copy of a letter from a gentleman of the Island of St. Vincent to the Rev. Mr Clarke, one of the Rev. Mr Wesley's Missionaries in the West Indies, containing a short History of the Caribs, Byrea, St. Vincent, July 24, 1787 by George Davidson.

Authentic Papers Relative to the Expedition against the Charibbs and the Sale of Lands in the Island of St. Vincent: London. Printed for J. Alamon opposite Burlington House in Piccadilly- MDCCLXXIII.

By Right Hon. P Grenville (1765 Survey Instructions) Original Instructions to the Commissions for the Sale of Lands in St. Vincent, 1765

GD (26) 28/2/1- AA 2.1.8 01197/8/1 (1-4): Sale of Lands. From A Narrative of General Melville's

Journey through the Islands – May-June-July.

Council Minutes – March 19, 1795, C.O 260/14

Authentic Papers Relative to the Expedition Against the Charaibs in the island of St. Vincent(MDCCIXXIII). "Letter from Lieutenant Governor Fitzmaurice to the Earl of Hillsborough, St. Vincent June 10, 1769."

St. Vincent Archives

SVG-RBC-269. "Official Declaration Conferring the Honour of National Hero, Saint Vincent and the Grenadines on the Right Excellent Paramount Chief of the Kalinago People, Joseph Chatoyer (mid 1700-mid 1795).

Newspapers

The News, Kingstown, March 8 & 15, 2002.

Searchlight, March 8 & 15, 2002; March 21, 2003; March 16, 2007.

The Vincentian, March 8 & 15, 2002; March 21, 2003.

www.ingramcontent.com/pod-product-compliance
Lightning Source LLC
LaVergne TN
LVHW041611070526
838199LV00052B/3093